Days of
Knights and Damsels

An Activity Guide

Laurie Carlson

CHICAGO REVIEW PRESS

Library of Congress Cataloging-in-Publication Data
Carlson, Laurie M., 1952-
     Days of knights and damsels : an activity guide / Laurie Carlson.
       p. cm.
     Originally published: Huzzah means hooray. — 1st ed. C1995.
     Includes bibliographical references (p. 173).
     Summary: More than 100 illustrated crafts, projects, and
games help recreate the culture and world of the Middle Ages, when
books were handmade and read by candlelight, sundials told the
hour, and going barefoot was illegal.
     ISBN 1-55652-291-6
     1. Handicraft-Juvenile literature. 2. Middle Ages—History—
Juvenile literature. 3. Civilization, Medieval—Juvenile literature.
4. Europe—Social life and customs—Juvenile literature.
[1. Handicraft. 2. Middle Ages-History. 3. Civilization,
Medieval. 4. Europe—Social life and customs.]
     I. Carlson, Laurie M., 1952- Huzzah means hooray. II. Title.
TT160.C353   1998
745.5—dc21   97-36359
                                                        CIP
                                                        AC
                                                     Rev.

Originally published as *Huzzah Means Hooray: Activities from the
Days of Damsels, Jesters, and Blackbirds in a Pie.*

The author and the publisher of this book disclaim all liability incurred
in connection with the use of the information contained in this book.

Interior illustrations by Sean O'Neill and Laurie Carlson
Typography by MobiGraphics, Inc., Chicago, Illinois

First edition
Published by Chicago Review Press, Incorporated
814 North Franklin Street
Chicago, Illinois 60610
ISBN 1-55652-291-6
Printed in the United States of America

5 4 3 2

Books were the most important creation
to come out of the Middle Ages. Libraries, too.
I'm thankful I don't have to visit a monastery or beg a king
to see the royal library. I thank *my* libraries for being there when I
want to find information. Be sure to visit *your* library.
Volunteer to help sort and shelve books, make posters,
donate old books and magazines.
Most of all, enjoy the books they keep for *all* of us to use.
Thank you: Coeur d'Alene Public Library, Hayden Lake Public
Library, University of Idaho Library, North Idaho College Library, and
Foley Center Library at Gonzaga University.
I'll be back, with book bag in hand!

Contents

Medieval—What's That?

Huzzah! That's how people said "Hooray!" in Europe long ago. It was in the days of knights and queens, castles and cottages. We call it the Middle Ages, or the *medieval* time.

For us today, *huzzah* is a funny word. It sounds a lot like "fuzz-SAW." The word *medieval* is pronounced "meed-evil."

The years were between 480 and 1500 A.D. It was a time span of about a thousand years and ended when Columbus and other explorers traveled to the rest of the world.

Europe was made up of many small countries and kingdoms then. The people lived under the rule of a king and queen or lord and lady, who owned the land. Kings and queens tried to rule more land by taking over their neighbors' kingdoms through war. During that time, people depended on one another for many things. Those who worked (the peasants) fed those who fought (the knights) and those who prayed (the monks). The fighters protected the kingdom, and the monks prayed for all.

The days of knights and castles were long ago, yet we still find them interesting. We can look at their books and paintings and see that their customs and beliefs were the beginnings of our own. People who traveled to the New World brought many customs and ways of living with them from their Old World homes. Their ideas about freedom, government, and religion formed the ways we do things in North America today. Their writing, schools, and art influenced ours. When we look back, we can see something of ourselves.

Many years ago, Europe was very different from today. During the Middle Ages, homes were castles (if you were rich and royal) or cottages (for everyone else). People lived in small towns around a castle, where they farmed or made things to trade with each other. The owner of the castle might have been a king or a rich and powerful knight who served the king.

Most people didn't travel very far because bandits and robbers would stop them, and the people in other kingdoms usually didn't speak the same language. It was a dangerous time to live because pirates, bandits, and attacking armies from other lands were always a threat. People lived near a castle so that the king's knights could protect them. Villages and castles had walls around them with gates. At night these gates were closed. Watchmen were assigned to spot travelers coming.

Explorers began traveling to other lands by the end of the Middle Ages. That's when Columbus made his journey to North America and Marco Polo explored far-off China.

> *In the Middle Ages, only neighboring villages could understand each other's language. If you traveled beyond three or four villages, you probably wouldn't understand the language. People worked hard and many died from sickness. At that time, no one knew what made people sick. They thought that illness was caused by smells or magic.*

People then had very simple lives, but they began reading and writing, trading goods in markets, and going to fairs where they saw new things, such as spices, silk fabric, and perfumes as well as jugglers, puppet shows, and plays.

Religion was very important. People went to the church or synagogue every day and prayed before they went to bed at night, in the morning when they got up, and before meals. Some people devoted their lives to the church, living together in monasteries as monks or nuns. There, they grew gardens, wrote books, and taught lessons to children. They cared for orphans and the poor.

As protection against evil spells, children wore pieces of coral on necklaces. Children of ordinary families had to begin working as soon as they could walk! They gathered sticks for firewood, picked berries, and collected the bits of wool that fell off of the sheep. As they got older, they were given jobs herding geese or pigs. Girls were hired out as maids when they were six years old. By the time children were 10 years old, they were working like adults.

Childhood—What Was It Like?

Long ago, babies caught illnesses easily and many didn't live very long.

Children in the castles were trained to do jobs, too. Girls were taught things that they needed to know for their job as lady of the castle when they married. They learned to plan meals and banquets, to heal the wounded, and to train young pages in good manners. Girls learned to sing and to play musical instruments so that they could entertain guests. They learned to ride horses expertly.

Wealthy girls were also expected to do fine needlework and to dress beautifully.

The sons of the castle families were trained to become knights. First, they worked as pages in another family's castle. Pages served and cleaned during banquets. When they were teenagers, they became squires to knights. They carried the knight's equipment at tournaments and battles and helped him with his horse and armor.

Rich or Poor, Peasant or Royal

Children also had time for toys, games, and singing. They played sports and raised pets, such as cats, dogs, and birds. They went to fairs to watch plays and puppet shows, or to tournaments to cheer for their favorite knight.

By the end of the Middle Ages, girls and boys of wealthy families were taught reading and writing by tutors or in schools. Parents read bedtime stories to their children and told them some of the same stories we still tell today.

> *Wealthy parents began teaching their children how to read and write before they were seven years old. Records tell of one girl who could read at the age of three!*

Let's Dress Up!

Clothes in the Middle Ages were loose and worn in layers. Everyone wore a long outer garment, stockings, a shirt, a jacket, and a gown or coat (no underwear!). In cold weather, a hooded cape was worn over everything. Rich and poor wore the same styles, but made from different cloth.

Peasants wore work clothing made of gray or brown homespun fabric. They had one outfit for dressing up on holidays. Royalty and rich people wore clothes made of fine fabrics dyed in beautiful colors. They enjoyed wearing fur, lace, ribbons, and lots of silver buttons or gold embroidery on their clothes. It was against the law for peasants to wear certain colors—such as purple—and their clothing could only have a limited number of buttons or trim. It was against the law for peasants to wear the fine things that the wealthy could.

Dresses had full skirts and fancy sleeves. One style of sleeves for ladies was so tight that the dress had to be stitched onto the woman each time it was worn! Brocade, gold ornaments, and embroidery made the clothing very fancy. People loved wearing finery and showing off their wealth. Laws were made to keep people from putting so much fancy trim on their clothes, but they didn't stop. Some fancy dresses cost as much as a large farm!

Clothes weren't sold in shops. If you were wealthy, a tailor made them for you from fabric you purchased. If you were a peasant, you made your clothes from fabric you wove at home out of wool taken from the family's sheep.

Because clothes were so hard to make, people wore them out; so they sewed on patches to make them last. Rich people gave their old clothes to the poor, and dealers sold old clothes at the markets.

> *Clothing decorated with points and bells along the edges was popular, but against the law—except for nobility or the wealthy. By the end of the Middle Ages, clothing was more elaborate.*

Medieval Outfit

Look through your family's closets (ask permission first) and put together an outfit for yourself. You can also find great costume pieces at yard sales and thrift shops—just like the old-clothes dealers in the medieval days!

You'll need to find long stockings or tights. Add a long robe or dress with a loose smock or vest over it.

Make a cape by pinning a sheet or towel at your shoulders or tying it at the neck.

Try on some leather boots or sandals over thick socks.

For boys, wear tights or pants with a long, loose smock-type shirt over them. Wear a belt at the waist and a cape tied at the neck.

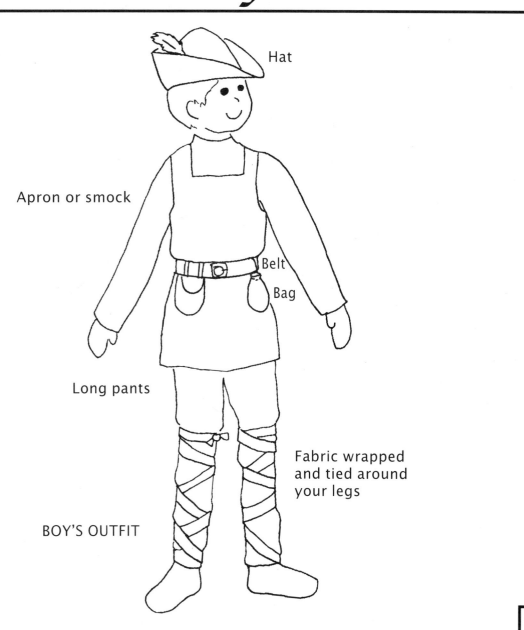

Hat

Apron or smock

Belt

Bag

Long pants

Fabric wrapped and tied around your legs

BOY'S OUTFIT

Fabric scarf

Ribbons tied
onto the
sleeves

Short jumper
over a long
dress

GIRL'S OUTFIT

Girls can wear a long dress and put on a shorter jumper or apron over it. If the dress doesn't have fancy sleeves, tie several ribbons around the sleeves.

A belt was also worn at the waist, over the clothing. Things were tied onto it: a bag, fan, looking glass, pomander, or metal drinking cup. Tuck your gloves in the belt when you aren't wearing them.

Everyone wore hats: felt hats, hats with veils, feathers, or other trim, headpieces made from scarves, or simple caps.

Tie on a hood.

Top a cloth circle with a crown.

Men sometimes wore twisted scarves wrapped around their heads.

Men's cap (German)

Girls wore flower garlands and long hair.

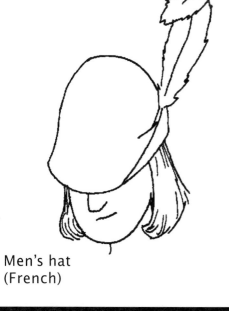

Men's hat (French)

Pin a veil to your hair.
Pin a cardboard headband over it.

Girl's headdress
(English)

Wig with Braids

Girls usually wore their hair long, in braids, or wrapped in coils above their ears. If you don't have long hair, make your own.

MATERIALS
Panty hose
Scissors
Ribbons
Needle and thread (optional)

Cut off the feet. Cut the legs into 3 sections.

Cut the foot sections off at the ankles. Cut each leg into 3 sections. Begin at the top and braid each leg. Try it on and adjust the braids. Tie ribbons at the ends. You can wrap the braids around in coils at the sides of your head and stitch them in place with a needle and thread.

Wear a hat, scarf, or veil over the wig.

Tie the braids with ribbons or coil them at the sides of your head.

Robin Hood's Cap

MATERIALS

Two, 9-by-16-inch felt pieces
Fabric glue or sewing machine
Scissors
Real or paper feather

Cut 2 triangles, 16 inches wide at the bottom and 9 inches tall. Use thick fabric glue or ask an adult to help you with a sewing machine. Glue or stitch the two edges of the cap together.

Fold the brim up in the back about 4 inches.

Snip 2 tiny slits and stick the feather through them.

(You can also make this cap from a large brown paper bag. Staple the edges instead of gluing.)

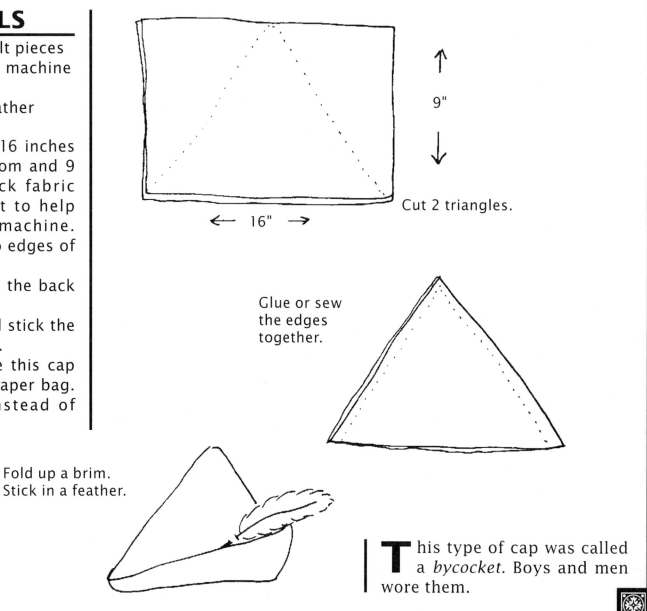

9"

16"

Cut 2 triangles.

Glue or sew the edges together.

Fold up a brim.
Stick in a feather.

This type of cap was called a *bycocket.* Boys and men wore them.

Princess Hat

It's easy to make a hat like the ones royal ladies wore long ago. This type of hat was called a *henin*.

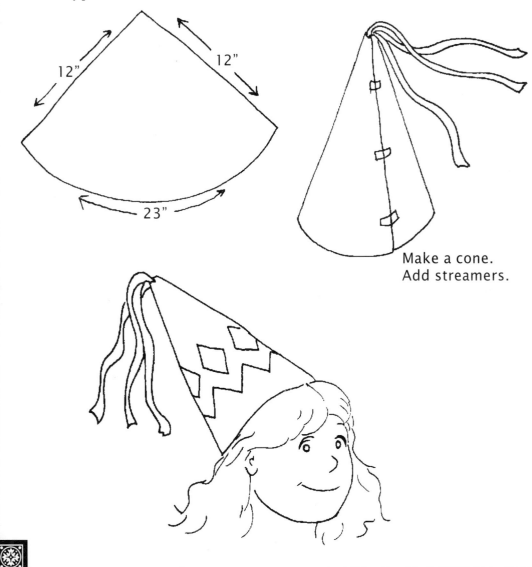

12"   12"

23"

Make a cone.
Add streamers.

MATERIALS

Posterboard, butcher paper, or large brown paper bags
Nylon net, crepe paper streamers, or ribbons
Pencil
Scissors
Markers, crayons, or glitter and glue
Glue or tape
Stapler
Hairpins

Draw and cut a large quarter circle. Use markers, crayons, or glitter and glue to decorate it with any designs you like.

Roll it into a cone that fits your head. Glue or tape it in place and staple to hold.

Cut a veil from nylon net, crepe paper streamers, or ribbons. Push the ends into the tip of the cone and glue or staple them in place.

Use hairpins to fasten the henin on your head.

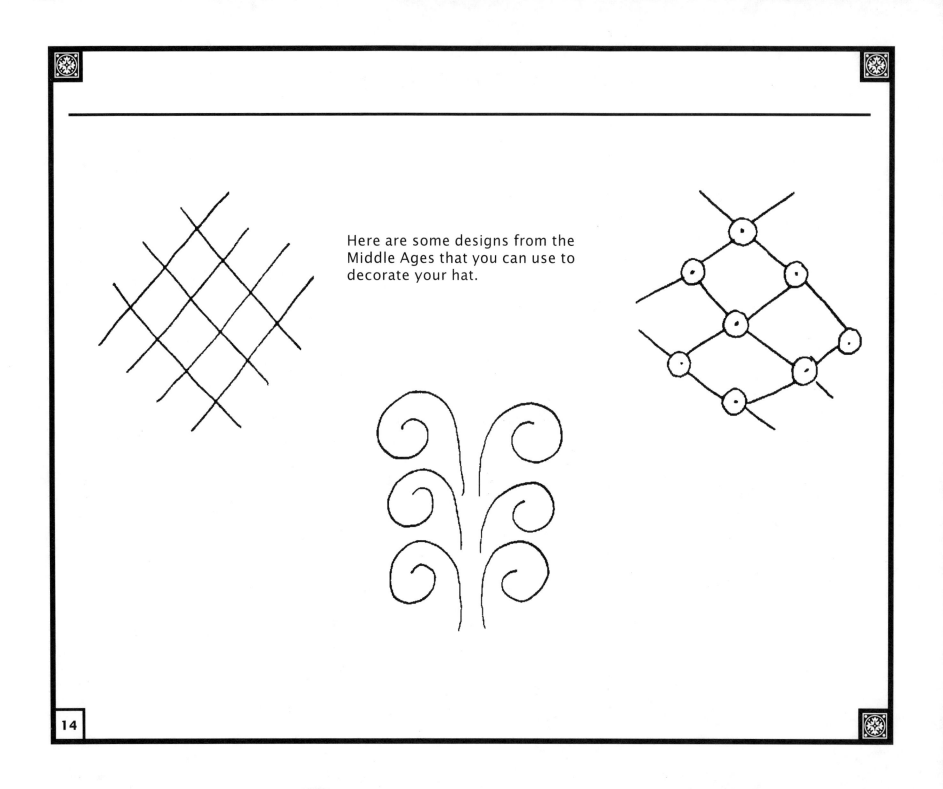

Here are some designs from the Middle Ages that you can use to decorate your hat.

Pocket & Almoner

MATERIALS

Two, 12-inch felt squares
Belt or cord
Scissors
Glue or a large sewing needle
and embroidery thread or
lightweight yarn
Sock
Yarn

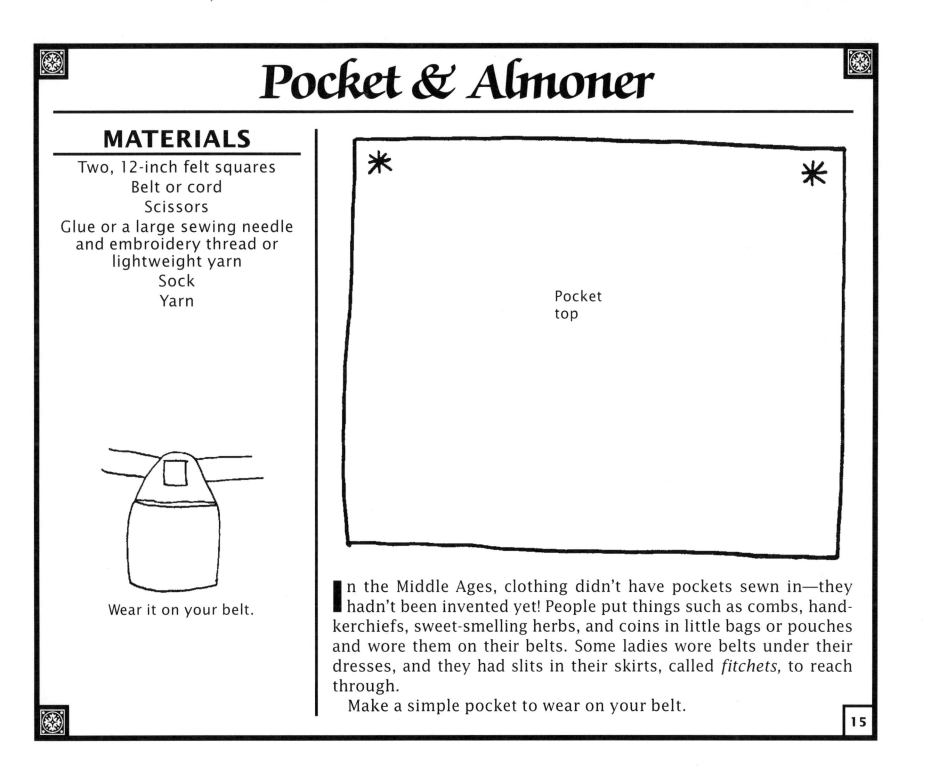

Wear it on your belt.

Pocket
top

In the Middle Ages, clothing didn't have pockets sewn in—they hadn't been invented yet! People put things such as combs, handkerchiefs, sweet-smelling herbs, and coins in little bags or pouches and wore them on their belts. Some ladies wore belts under their dresses, and they had slits in their skirts, called *fitchets,* to reach through.

Make a simple pocket to wear on your belt.

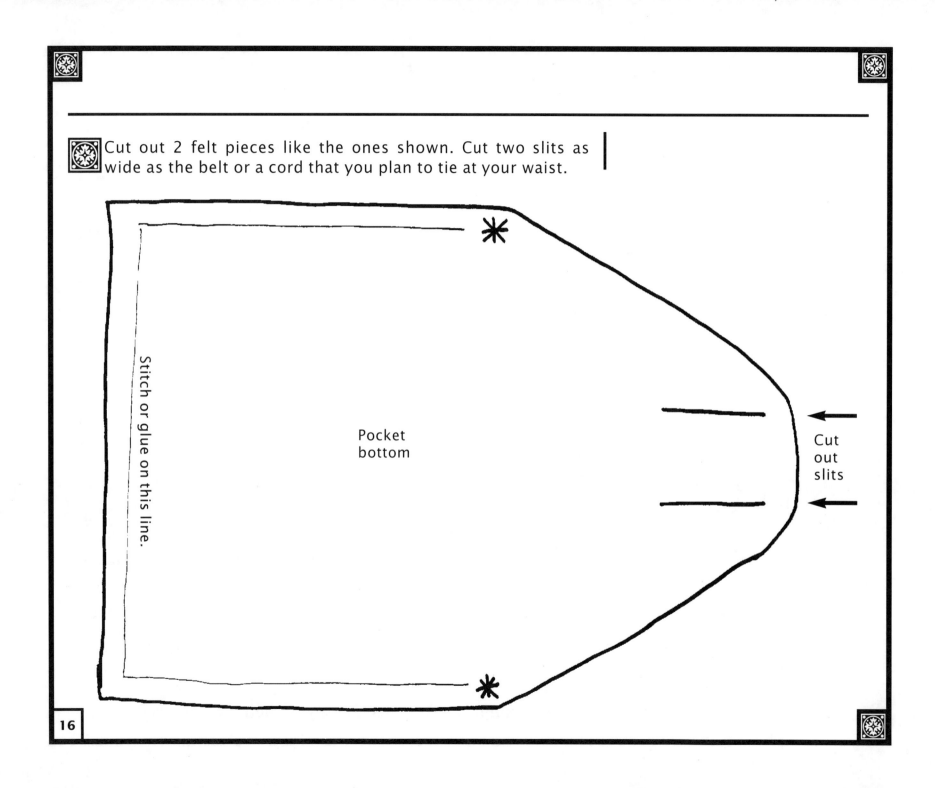

Cut out 2 felt pieces like the ones shown. Cut two slits as wide as the belt or a cord that you plan to tie at your waist.

Stitch or glue on this line.

Pocket bottom

Cut out slits

Lay the smaller piece on top of the larger one and glue around the outer edge, or stitch it by hand. A nice stitch to use is the buttonhole stitch (see the drawing).

You can decorate your pocket with embroidery (see p. 127 for embroidery) or by gluing on pieces of felt.

People also wore a sock-like bag called an *almoner*. They kept money in it, called *alms,* to give to street beggars. Tie the top of a sock closed with a length of yarn, and then loop and tie it onto your belt.

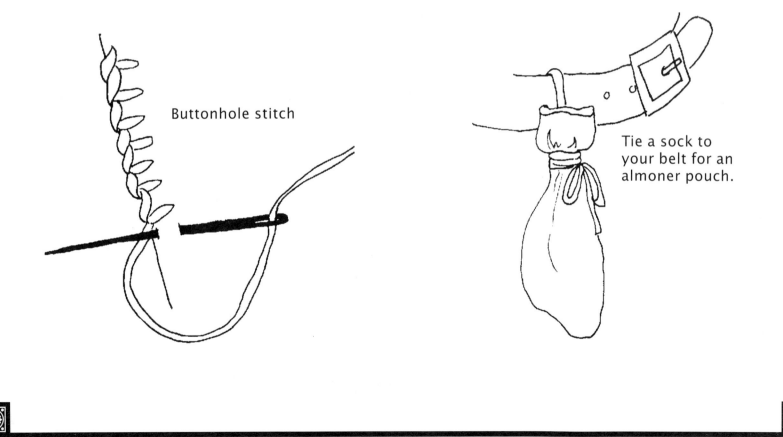

Buttonhole stitch

Tie a sock to your belt for an almoner pouch.

Lady's Looking Glass

The first mirrors were made of polished tin. Later, glass was painted with silver to make mirrors like the ones we use now.

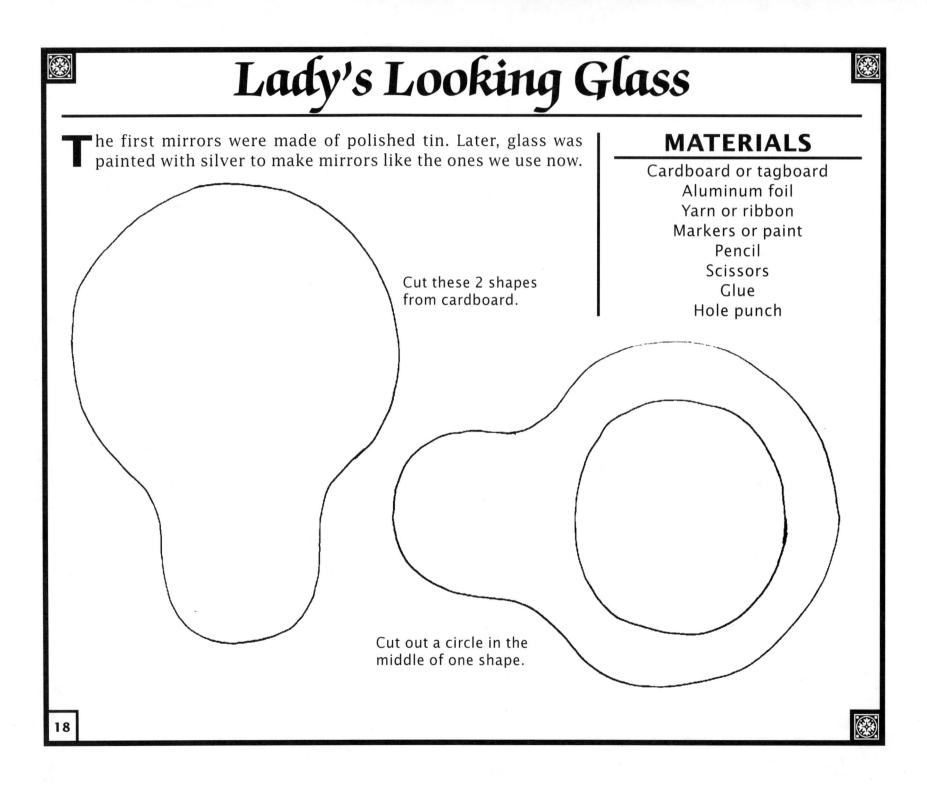

Cut these 2 shapes from cardboard.

Cut out a circle in the middle of one shape.

MATERIALS
Cardboard or tagboard
Aluminum foil
Yarn or ribbon
Markers or paint
Pencil
Scissors
Glue
Hole punch

Trace the two shapes from the illustration onto the cardboard and cut them out. Decorate them with markers or paint.

Cut out a piece of foil large enough to fill the cutout circle in the first piece. Glue it to the other cardboard piece, with the *shiny* side facing you. Glue the cardboard piece with the cutout circle on top.

Punch a hole in the end so that you can tie the looking glass to your belt with yarn or ribbon. You can also pin it to your tunic or vest or wear it on a string tied around your neck.

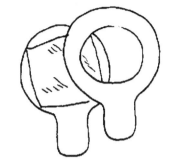

Glue foil between them.

You can make easy tracing patterns from this book: Save the heavy clear-plastic bag inside a cold cereal box. Cut it open flat, lay it over the page, and trace lines with a permanent felt-tipped marker.

String it from your belt.

Shoes

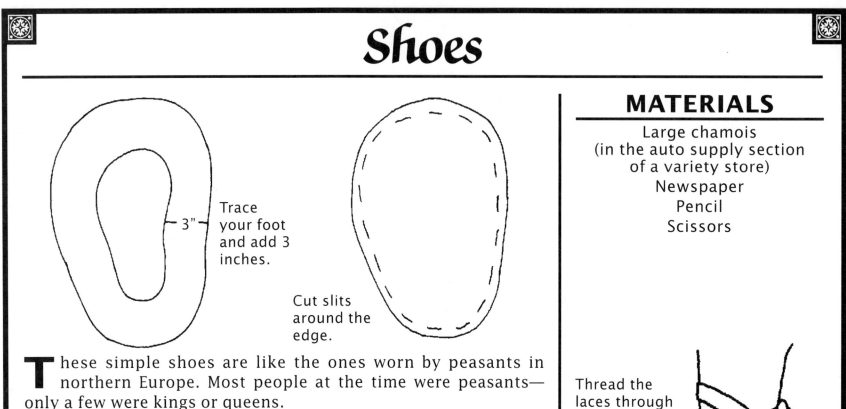

—3"—

Trace your foot and add 3 inches.

Cut slits around the edge.

MATERIALS

Large chamois
(in the auto supply section
of a variety store)
Newspaper
Pencil
Scissors

These simple shoes are like the ones worn by peasants in northern Europe. Most people at the time were peasants—only a few were kings or queens.

Trace your foot onto the newspaper. Add 3 inches all around your foot pattern. Cut it out. Lay the pattern on the chamois, trace around it, and cut it out. Make two.

Cut ½-inch slits around the edge of the shoe, about 1 inch apart.

Use the rest of the chamois for laces. You can make laces from the scraps by cutting them out in a spiral. First, trim the corners of a larger scrap of chamois so that it is rounded. Cut a strip half an inch wide by starting at the outside edge and cutting around and around until you reach the center. Make two long laces, knotting pieces together if you need to.

Thread the laces through the slits. Crisscross them around your foot and tie them at the back of your ankle.

Thread the laces through the slits, and then wrap and tie them.

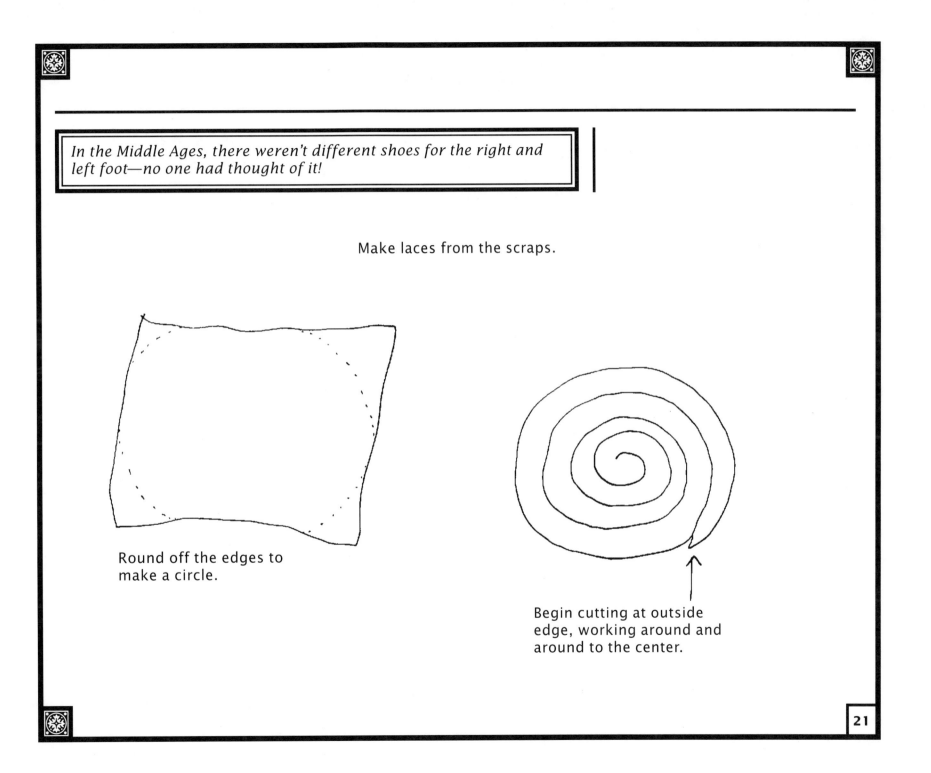

In the Middle Ages, there weren't different shoes for the right and left foot—no one had thought of it!

Make laces from the scraps.

Round off the edges to make a circle.

Begin cutting at outside edge, working around and around to the center.

Poulaines

Poulaines were shoes with very long, pointy toes. Some had points so long that a special wooden sandal was worn underneath to support them.

Make a really simple version of poulaines for your medieval costume:

MATERIALS

Construction paper
Yarn
Pencil
Scissors
Hole punch

Draw and cut out a long, pointy shape that fits the top of your foot. Trace it to make another just like it for the other foot.

Trim the short end so it curves a little to fit your ankle. Punch 6 holes across the bottom as shown. Thread a length of yarn through the holes.

Lay the paper poulaines on top of your real shoes and tie them around your ankle. If your points are long, curl them upward to make walking easier.

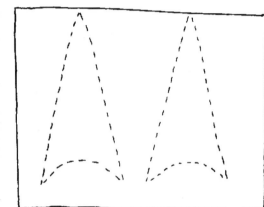

Cut 2 long, pointy shapes.

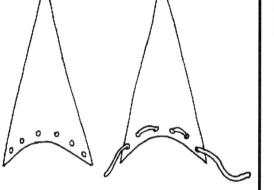

Trim the flat end to curve a bit. Punch holes and thread laces through.

Tie them on over your shoes.

Cloak

MATERIALS

Large brown paper bag
Yarn
Scissors
Pencil
Hole punch
Masking tape

Fasten with a yarn tie or a chain from some old jewelry.

Cloaks, or capes, were worn throughout most of Europe during the Middle Ages. Some were lined with fur for warmth.

Cut down one side of a large brown paper bag. Cut away the bottom of the bag. Open it flat and trim the corners to make a half-circle. Cut out a half-circle for the neck.

Put masking tape at the corners of the neck to keep the paper from tearing. Punch holes through it and tie with a length of yarn.

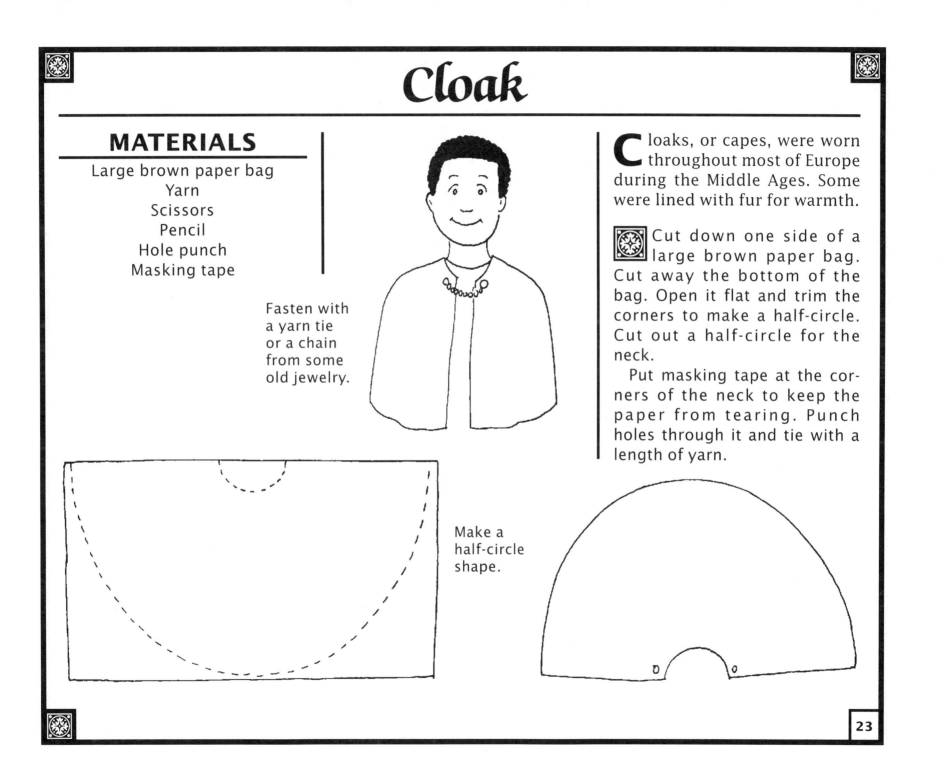

Make a half-circle shape.

Paper Ruff

MATERIALS

2 sheets 8½-by-11-inch paper
Scissors
Glue
Safety pins

 Cut the sheets of paper in half lengthwise to make 4 pieces. Glue the ends together to make 1 long strip. Fold the strip accordion-style, creasing it back and forth. Make the folds about as wide as your finger.

Put it around your neck and adjust it. Pin the ends together or to your collar.

Ruffs were collars made of stiff, pleated fabric. Both men and women wore them. Ruffs were so popular among the wealthy of the time that many women earned a living by washing and starching them.

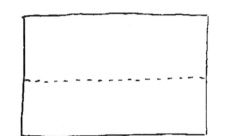 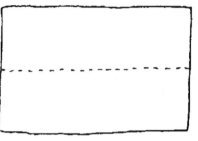

Cut into 4 pieces.

Glue them together to make 1 long strip.

Fold the strip accordion-style.

Crowns, Tiaras & Garlands

Crowns were symbols for how important a king or queen was. They were made of gold or silver and decorated with precious stones. A king or queen also held a royal mace and sword as symbols of his or her power.

Royalty displayed these lavish treasures, along with their gold and silver dishes, jewels, and books, to impress visitors from other kingdoms. The more treasures they could show off, the more powerful they were thought to be.

You can make a crown from a strip of colored paper. Cut and decorate it with markers or glue and glitter. Staple the ends together to fit your head.

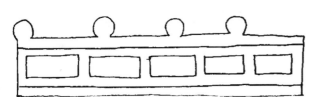

German-style crown made out of paper.

Cut a crown from the milk jug's center. Decorate it with permanent markers.

Glue pom pons to the points.

25

A girl's tiara can be cut from the top of a plastic gallon milk jug. Punch holes at the ends and tie on 2 pieces of yarn to tie the tiara onto your head.

Cut this shape from the side of a plastic jug.

Punch holes, decorate, and tie on yarn.

Tie around your head.

Young girls often wore garlands of flowers in their hair. You can make one with thin, floral wire and some old silk flowers with the stems cut short.

Bend one piece of wire to fit your head. With another piece of wire, wrap the short stems of the flowers to the first wire. Tie ribbons to the sides or back.

Loop the ribbons onto the wire.

Fit for a princess!

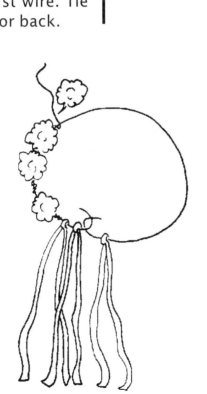

Bend the wire to fit your head. With another wire, wrap the flowers to it.

27

Royal Mace

MATERIALS

Long, paper tube
(from gift wrap or
paper towels)
Colored paper
Scissors
Stapler
Glue
Markers

Glue the colored paper to cover the tube. Cut 2 strips of paper, about 8 inches long and 1 inch wide. Staple them together in the center to make an "X." Glue the ends of the "X" across from each other at one end of the tube. Cut and glue another strip of colored paper over the ends to hide them.

Decorate with markers and brightly colored paper. Cut the paper into small shapes that look like jewels and precious stones. Glue them onto the handle of the mace. Now you're ready to hold court!

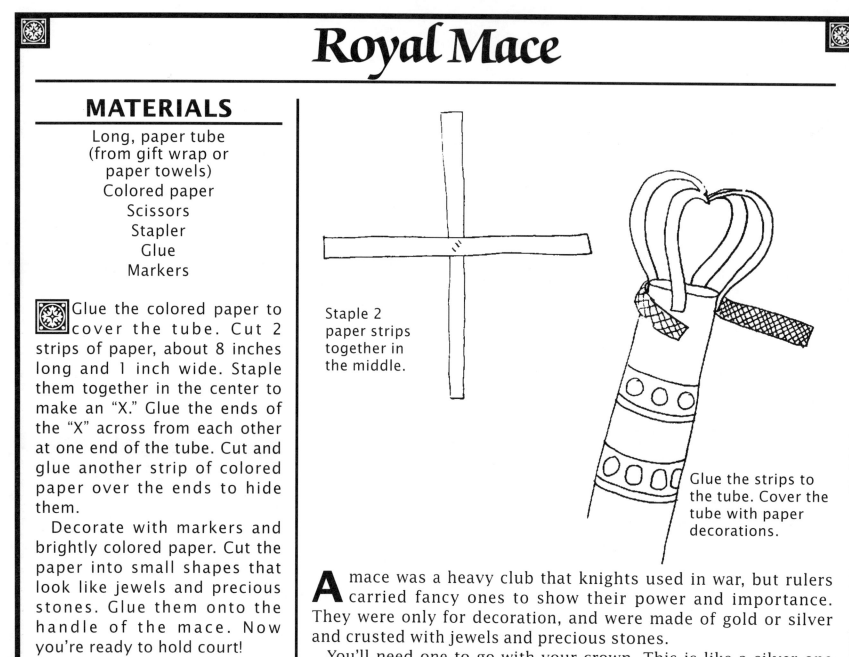

Staple 2 paper strips together in the middle.

Glue the strips to the tube. Cover the tube with paper decorations.

A mace was a heavy club that knights used in war, but rulers carried fancy ones to show their power and importance. They were only for decoration, and were made of gold or silver and crusted with jewels and precious stones.

You'll need one to go with your crown. This is like a silver one used in Ireland long ago.

Magic Wand

There weren't really any magical fairies in the Middle Ages, but people thought (or hoped) there were. We still like to tell stories that were told then—exciting tales of fairies granting wishes. Here's a quick and simple wand if you want to grant wishes of your own, or turn people into frogs!

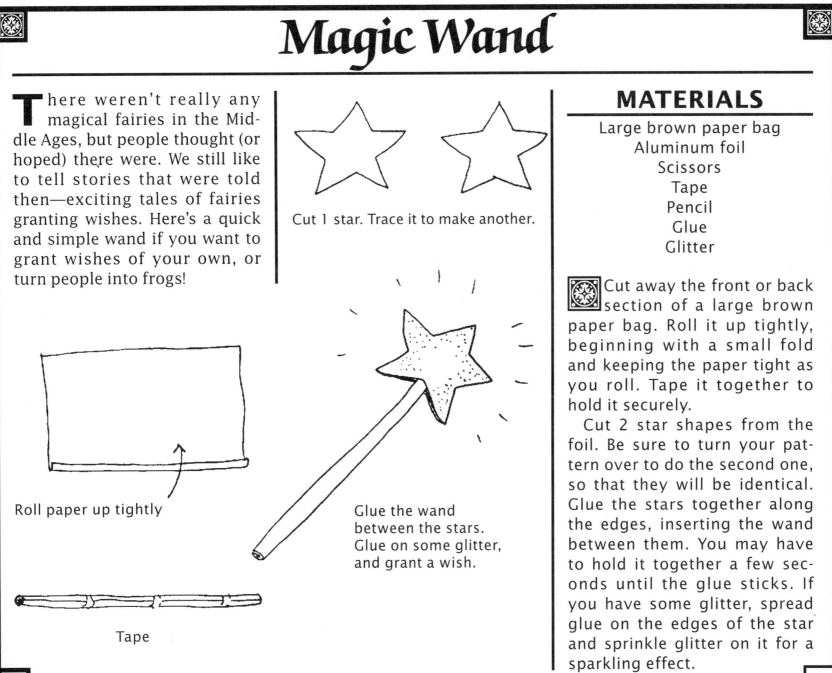

Cut 1 star. Trace it to make another.

Roll paper up tightly

Tape

Glue the wand between the stars. Glue on some glitter, and grant a wish.

MATERIALS

Large brown paper bag
Aluminum foil
Scissors
Tape
Pencil
Glue
Glitter

Cut away the front or back section of a large brown paper bag. Roll it up tightly, beginning with a small fold and keeping the paper tight as you roll. Tape it together to hold it securely.

Cut 2 star shapes from the foil. Be sure to turn your pattern over to do the second one, so that they will be identical. Glue the stars together along the edges, inserting the wand between them. You may have to hold it together a few seconds until the glue sticks. If you have some glitter, spread glue on the edges of the star and sprinkle glitter on it for a sparkling effect.

Buttons & Bracelets

MATERIALS

Buttons in lots of colors
and shapes
Elastic thread
Large-eyed darning needle
Scissors
Old barrettes, pins, earrings,
or hair combs
Glue

In Italy, there were laws to keep ordinary folks from copying the wealthy nobility. The height of towers on homes, the number of women at a wedding, and the value of wedding gifts were all set by law. Clothing laws were set, too. The number of jewels, belts, buttons, embroidery, fur, and fringe that could be worn was set by law.

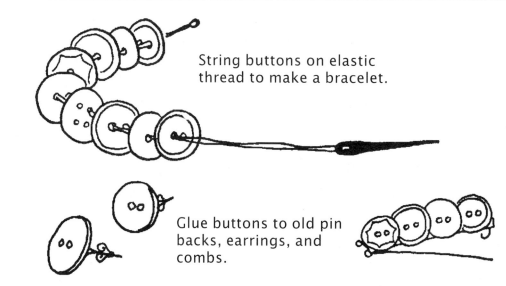

String buttons on elastic thread to make a bracelet.

Glue buttons to old pin backs, earrings, and combs.

Buttons were so popular that there were laws to keep people from wearing so many on their clothing that they might be mistaken for royalty. One royal child's garment had 170 silver buttons sewn on it!

Since buttons aren't against the law today, you can wear as many as you like. You can even make jewelry from them!

Create your own special bracelets. First, choose the buttons you want to use, thread the needle with a double length of elastic thread, and knot the end. String buttons on the thread until there are enough to fit around your wrist comfortably. Go back and thread the needle through the first couple of buttons again and knot the end of the thread securely.

Make more jewelry by gluing buttons to an old barrette back or pin back with tacky-type glue. You can glue them to earrings and hair combs. Look around and you'll find other ideas, too.

Knight's Armor

Knights fought to keep the kingdom safe from other kings' armies who tried to take over. The knights were very important to a king because he wanted to keep his power and his land. They also protected the peasants of the kingdom from being killed or taken prisoner and sold as slaves by enemies.

Boys trained as pages for years and then became squires who helped knights. Squires lived in the castle with one another and took turns at the many duties. They spent their time training to ride horses and fight when they weren't taking care of the horses, harnesses, weapons, and armor. When a knight went into battle at a tournament or war, the squire went at his side to help him.

Knights wore special clothing to protect them from lances, swords, and arrows in battle. A suit was made of *chain mail,* small metal rings that interlocked to make a mesh that arrows couldn't break through. A complete coat of mail covered a knight from head to knee. Each small link was made by hand and fastened to the others. A coat of mail contained thousands of links; so, of course, it was very expensive. One suit could cost a small farm. Armor was passed down from father to son and used for many years.

A suit of chain mail was heavy. It weighed as much as a child. It had to be worn for hours, and the knight also had to throw heavy lances and use battle axes and clubs while wearing it. Knights had to practice and exercise a lot to keep in shape for fighting.

Heavy metal plates were shaped and fastened together to make armor that knights wore over their chain mail. Armor was also made for horses, and even dogs!

Perhaps you live near a museum that has real medieval armor on display.

> *The squire cleaned the knight's armor by rubbing it with sand and vinegar. This kept the armor from rusting.*

Helmet

There were many different kinds of helmets. Be sure you make large eye openings so you can see out while you're wearing it.

MATERIALS

Plastic gallon milk jug
Scissors
Hole punch

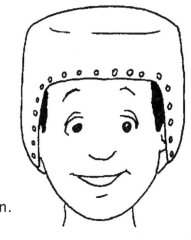Cut the jug as shown in the drawings. There are 2 styles to choose from. Punch holes along the edges or around the eye holes for decoration. You can make up other helmet ideas of your own, too.

Punch holes for decoration.

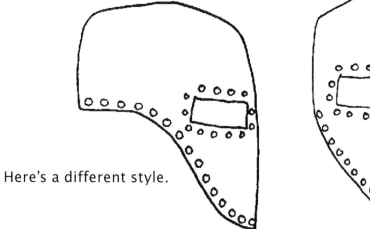

Here's a different style.

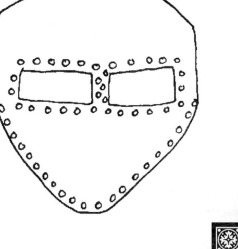

MATERIALS

Cardboard

Scissors

Paint, or colored paper and glue

Large nail or sharp pencil

Two 12-inch lengths of heavy cord

Shield

Knights used shields to protect themselves from lances and clubs.

Knights couldn't be recognized when they were covered with armor and helmets, so they decorated their shields with their family colors and designs, called a *coat of arms* (see p. 66 to make yours).

In the Middle Ages, shields were made of hides stretched over wooden frames, thin sheets of wood glued together, or metal. Shields fell apart during fighting, so a knight's squire carried several extra shields with them on a pack horse.

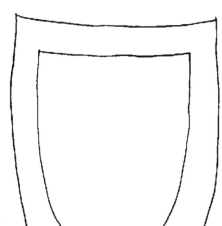
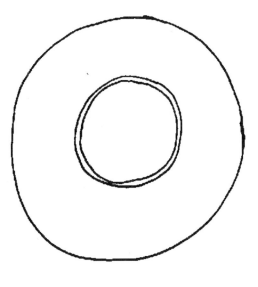
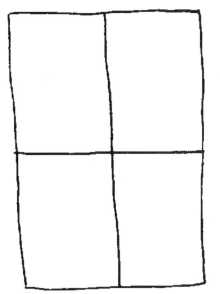

Shields came in many different shapes.

Cut the cardboard into whatever shape you like. Shields were shaped like circles, ovals, rectangles or curved triangles. Glue colored paper or paint a design on your shield that means something special to you.

Make 2 straps to hold the shield on your arm. Use a large nail or sharp pencil to punch 4 holes near the center of the shield as shown. Thread one length of cord through 2 holes that are next to each other and knot the ends to make loops. Do the same with the other length of cord and the remaining holes. Slide your arm through the first loop and grasp the second one with your hand. Bend your elbow to carry the shield in front of you.

Use cardboard to draw and cut out a sword. They were in many different shapes and sizes because each was handmade.

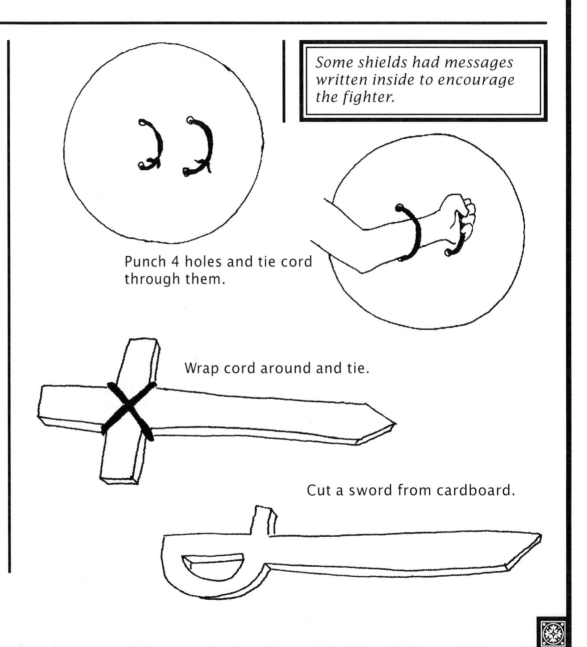

Some shields had messages written inside to encourage the fighter.

Punch 4 holes and tie cord through them.

Wrap cord around and tie.

Cut a sword from cardboard.

MATERIALS

3 plastic gallon milk jugs
Scissors
Hole punch
4 metal fasteners

Cut the side from 2 jugs for the front and back pieces.

Chest Armor

Cut the pieces from the jugs as shown in the illustration. Punch holes and fasten the shoulder pieces to the front and back pieces. Use metal fasteners that spread apart to hold, but be sure that you put the head of the fastener *inside* the armor, so the ends don't poke you.

To put the armor on just drop it down over your head.

You can also use other jugs and 2-liter plastic bottles to make up armor to tie onto your arms and legs.

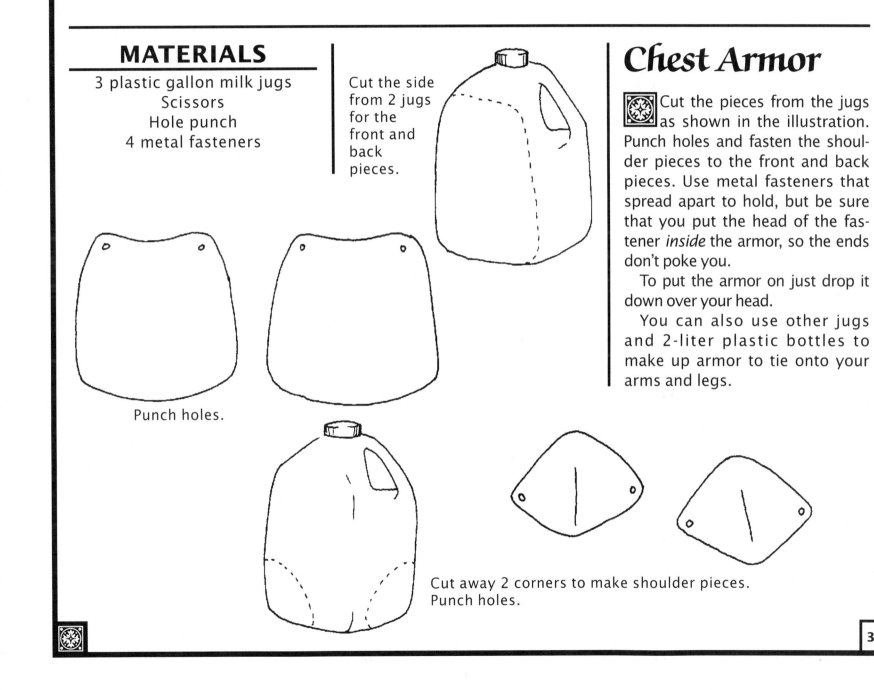

Punch holes.

Cut away 2 corners to make shoulder pieces. Punch holes.

After serving years as a page and squire, a man could be knighted. The ceremony began with a bath, dressing in white clothing, and a night of prayer in church. After Mass and a feast, a knight was dubbed with the gift of a sword and three taps on the shoulder by the king.

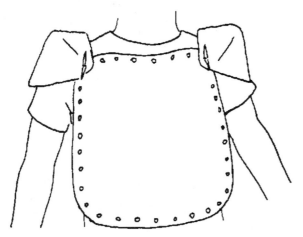

Fasten the front and back to the shoulders with metal fasteners.

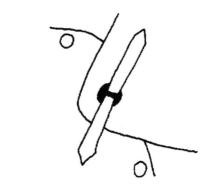

Spread the arms of the fasteners outside the armor.

Lady's Favors

Knights enjoyed fighting in tournaments. It gave them a chance to show off their skills and win prizes. The winning knight often won the losing knight's horse, too.

Ladies who watched the tournament gave *favors* to their favorite knight to help bring him good luck. These favors were small handkerchiefs, flowers, or ribbons that the knight could tie to his flag or pin to his tunic.

You can make your own favors to wear in your hair, use as a bookmark, or give to your favorite knight!

MATERIALS

Scraps of lace or woven trim
Narrow ribbons
Small silk flower
Needle and thread
Scissors
Glue

Thread the needle and knot the ends together. Stitch one edge of the lace with long, straight stitches. Pull the stitches tight and knot securely. Sew the ends together to make a rosette.

Cut several lengths of ribbon about 6 inches long. Glue them to the back of the rosette. Glue a silk flower to the center of the rosette.

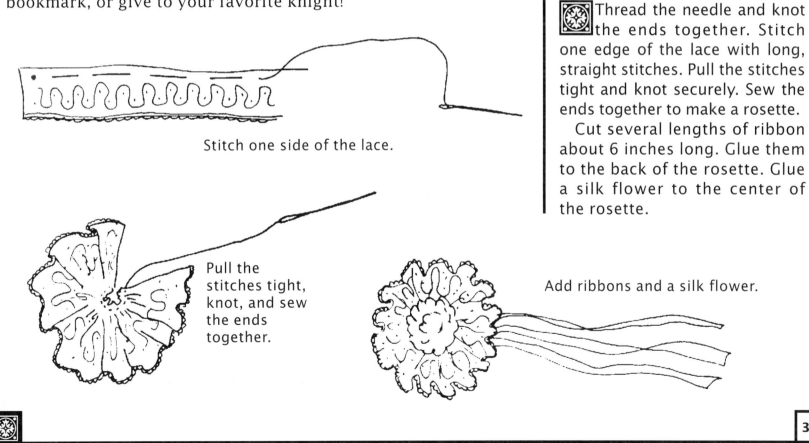

Stitch one side of the lace.

Pull the stitches tight, knot, and sew the ends together.

Add ribbons and a silk flower.

Time to Eat!

The kinds of meals and the way they were eaten were a bit different a thousand years ago. People ate plants they grew or animals they raised. Peasants had small gardens for their family and the castle had large gardens and orchards. Whether they were rich or poor, everyone in the Middle Ages had much the same foods to eat: milk, cheese, eggs, nuts, fruits such as apples, pears, and cherries, fresh vegetables from the garden such as peas, beans, and cabbage, and whatever salted meat they had preserved. Since the wealthy people owned the land, they were the only ones who could hunt there. Peasants were punished for hunting on royal land, but could usually fish in the streams.

Even peasants living in town kept animals. They tied their cow by the door, using the milk for cheese, curds, and butter. Their pigs and hens roamed freely. The streets were muddy and full of garbage, and the pigs actually helped by eating the waste.

Peasants usually ate dark bread or porridge, cabbage, bacon, and a helping of curds to top off a meal. They had eggs when the hens were laying, and fruits and vegetables from the garden in the summer.

People stored as much food as they could in chests and storerooms, often up to two years' supply. They kept meat from spoiling by packing it in salt. It was important to have a stock of food in case there were crop failures or harsh winters, and without money or stores, the peasants couldn't buy food if they ran out.

The poor ate mostly bread and leftovers given out at the castle gate. Records tell us that very poor people sometimes had to live on meals of grass, walnuts, acorns, and bread made from tree bark.

Feasts

Whenever there was a wedding, a knighting ceremony, or a visit from other royalty, a feast was held in the castle. These festivities were held in the warm months, when food was available. Lots of food was prepared, and served in course after course.

The rich people ate pretty much the same food as the poor, but they had a lot more of it, and the cooks had time to prepare it in fancy or interesting ways. Here is a common menu from a feast: white and brown bread and butter, wine, roast pig, chicken, goose, meat and vegetable pies, soups, puddings, and fish. Desserts were pears, apples, grapes, cheese, gingerbread, and wafers (cookies). Things weren't served in a special order; a dessert might come first, then two meat dishes, and then soup.

Castle cooks spent time and effort creating fancy feasts using simple foods. Foods at a feast weren't cooked to taste better; instead, they were served in huge quantities and fixed in unusual ways to surprise and entertain the guests. Fruits and vegetables were cut into unusual shapes. Exotic birds, such as peacocks, were served with their feathers stuck into a pastry coating for decoration. Swans were cooked and served whole.

If you want to have a medieval feast, here's an easy-to-fix menu using today's foods:

Canned ham (sliced)
Frozen chicken pies
Raw carrots, celery, and radishes cut into interesting shapes
Beef stew
Hard-boiled eggs
Rye or white bread and butter
Sliced cheeses
Turnips or parsnips
Lentils
Drinks: Lemonade, apple or berry juice, or milk
Dessert: Sliced pound cake spread with honey or jam, fruit pudding

> *Food was scarce in the winter. Even rich people ate only beans and porridge then. During a famine, the poor might eat only grass.*

Proper Manners

People ate with spoons, cutting their food with their own knives that they kept in sheaths on their belts. Forks were only used for cooking or serving food. No one used napkins; so, before and after eating, bowls of water and small towels were passed around the table so that everyone could wash their hands.

At royal feasts, it was the custom for two people to share serving platters of food, and to drink from one cup between them.

Meals weren't eaten off of plates. Instead, a piece of hard bread, called a *trencher,* was used. It was laid on the table, and meat or stew was eaten off of it. When the meal was finished, the trencher was eaten, too. The wealthy didn't eat their trenchers, though. The trenchers were gathered up after meals and given to the poor who waited outside to eat them.

Rise & Shine Breakfast

The lord and lady of the castle ate this sort of breakfast, and so did their children: a trencher (slab of bread) with beef or mutton on it, small loaves of bread, and beer or wine to drink.

There wasn't any coffee or tea then, and many people didn't drink milk because it couldn't be kept cold. The drinking water was dirty and tasted bad, so even children drank beer with their meals.

Water was prepared for drinking by boiling it, then mixing in licorice, honey, or wine. (See how to make mead, on p. 62.) As more people became Christians, they began to drink wine instead of beer.

Basic Bread

Loaf from the 9th century

Slice the top of the dough with a knife before letting the dough rise.

Oval loaf from the 15th century

The price and weight of bread sold by the baker was set by law. If a dishonest baker was caught selling too small a loaf, he was punished by being dragged down the street with the loaf tied around his neck. People could throw whatever they wished at him.

Everyone ate bread at every meal. The flour that it was made from was ground from wheat or rye grains.

Usually there was only one oven in the village. The peasants didn't have much firewood because the forests were owned by the family in the castle, who used the firewood for their own ovens. Women made up their bread dough at home and carried it to the town baker to be cooked. The baker made and sold bread, too. The bread was shaped in round loaves, with slashes across the top.

Every time they made a batch of bread, women saved a bit of raw dough, kept it warm, and added it to the next batch of dough. This bit of dough made tiny air bubbles in the dough and gave the bread a light, fluffy texture. This is the same way we make sourdough bread today.

You can use frozen bread dough to shape loaves like they used to make. Thaw the dough and shape it into one round loaf, or one large round with two smaller ones beside it. Use a knife to make slashes across the top of the loaf. Let it rise and bake it following the package directions. Use your loaf to make a trencher, or make some butter (p.47) to go with it.

Try a Trencher

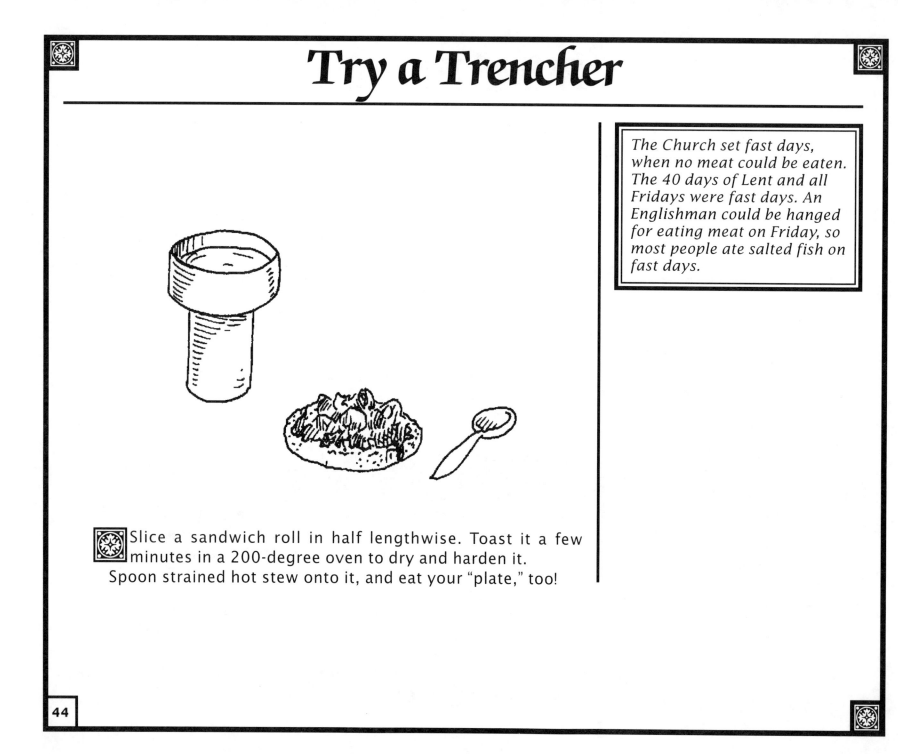

The Church set fast days, when no meat could be eaten. The 40 days of Lent and all Fridays were fast days. An Englishman could be hanged for eating meat on Friday, so most people ate salted fish on fast days.

Slice a sandwich roll in half lengthwise. Toast it a few minutes in a 200-degree oven to dry and harden it. Spoon strained hot stew onto it, and eat your "plate," too!

Smothered Bread

We call it *French* toast, but it was eaten by people all over Europe. People gathered eggs from their chickens, and milk from their cow or goat.

Soak the bread in the egg.

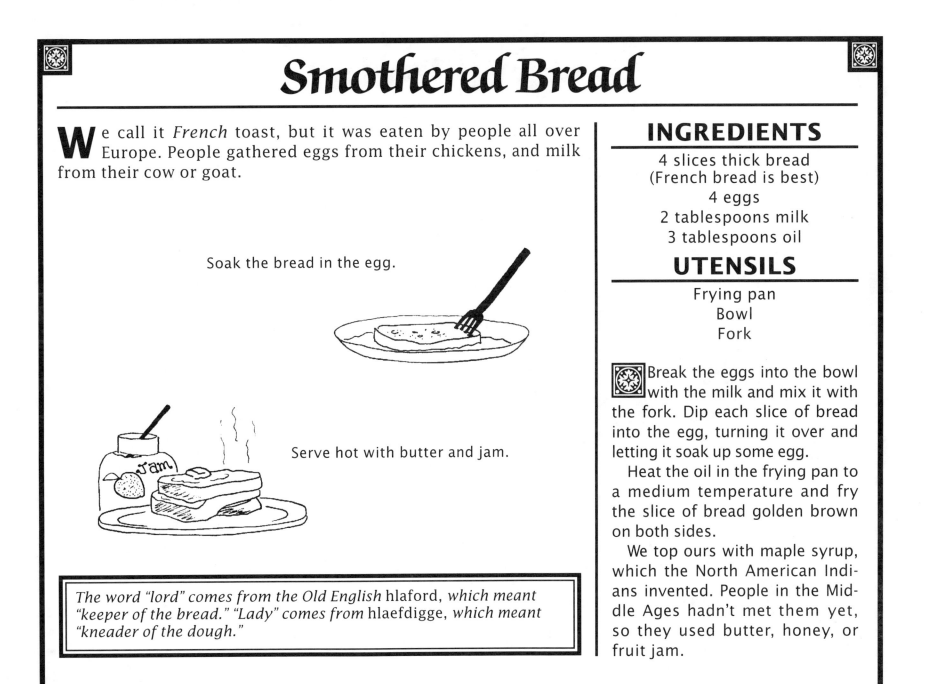

Serve hot with butter and jam.

The word "lord" comes from the Old English hlaford, *which meant "keeper of the bread." "Lady" comes from* hlaefdigge, *which meant "kneader of the dough."*

INGREDIENTS

4 slices thick bread
(French bread is best)
4 eggs
2 tablespoons milk
3 tablespoons oil

UTENSILS

Frying pan
Bowl
Fork

Break the eggs into the bowl with the milk and mix it with the fork. Dip each slice of bread into the egg, turning it over and letting it soak up some egg.

Heat the oil in the frying pan to a medium temperature and fry the slice of bread golden brown on both sides.

We top ours with maple syrup, which the North American Indians invented. People in the Middle Ages hadn't met them yet, so they used butter, honey, or fruit jam.

Twist a Pretzel

INGREDIENTS

1 package dry yeast
1 cup warm water
¼ cup sugar
1 teaspoon salt
2 tablespoons shortening
2 eggs
4 cups flour
2 tablespoons water
Salt
Sesame seeds

UTENSILS

Mixing bowl
Measuring cups and spoons
Mixing spoon
Greased cookie sheet
Pastry brush
(or a folded paper towel)
Paper towels

Pretzels were first given to children as rewards for learning to say their prayers correctly.

People used to make wishes on this twisted bread. Two people would hook their fingers through the loops, make silent wishes, and pull. The one who pulled off the largest piece might have his or her wish come true.

Grease the cookie sheet with shortening. Put the warm water and yeast in the bowl, and stir it until the yeast dissolves. Stir in the sugar, salt, shortening, 1 egg, and 2 cups of the flour. Mix until the batter is smooth.

Add the rest of the flour. Mix it with your hands to make a nice soft dough. Divide the dough into 2 pieces. Then, divide each piece into 8 lumps. Roll each lump between your hands to make a thin rope about 20 inches long. Arrange the ropes on the cookie sheet in a pretzel shape.

Cover the pretzels with paper towels and let them sit for 30 minutes while the yeast makes the dough rise and double in size.

Bake in a 370-degree oven for about 15 minutes. This will make 16 pretzels.

Beat the last egg with 2 tablespoons of water. Brush this mixture on top of the pretzels with a pastry brush. Sprinkle them with salt and sesame seeds.

Roll a rope of dough between your hands.

Twist into a pretzel shape.

Shake Up Some Butter

Medieval butter makers used churns, which looked like wooden buckets with wooden paddles inside, to stir the cream and make butter. You can use a glass jar.

Fill ⅓ to ½ of the jar with whipping cream. (½ pint of cream is enough for a mayonnaise jar. The same amount can also be divided into 3 baby food jars if you have friends to help with this project.)

Screw the jar lid on tightly and begin shaking the jar. Keep shaking the jar back and forth until the cream thickens, and then turns to butter. It will turn into a solid yellow ball, and the thin "buttermilk" will separate from it.

As you shake, you can chant, "Come, butter, come!" just like butter churners did long ago. Moving the jar back and forth works best. It takes less than 10 minutes.

Pat the butter into a round shape on a small plate. It's ready to eat on toast or crackers. Store it in the refrigerator.

Half a pint of cream makes about as much butter as there is in one cube from the store.

INGREDIENTS

½ pint whipping cream

UTENSILS

Glass jar with lid

A family's cow provided many of the basic foods they ate every day, including:

butter	*whey*
cream	*buttermilk*
cheese	*curds*
milk	

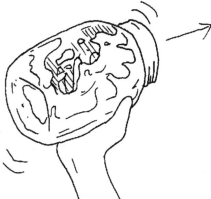

Shake the jar of cream back and forth until a ball of butter forms.

Spread it on toast or crackers.

Curds & Whey

INGREDIENTS

2 cups milk
(whole or 2 percent)
1 tablespoon white vinegar
Dash of salt
1 tablespoon cream

UTENSILS

Small pot
Cooking spoon
Strainer or colander

Curds were the perfect ending for almost any peasant's meal. They were like the cottage cheese we eat today. Even Little Miss Muffet ate them while sitting on her tuffet!

Add 1 tablespoon vinegar to the bubbling milk.

Pour the curds into a strainer to drain.

Heat the milk in the pot over medium heat until the milk begins to bubble. Take the pot off the stove and stir in the vinegar. Let it sit a few minutes and the milk will curdle. Pour it into the strainer and let the liquid (called *whey*) drain off the curds.

Chill the curds in the refrigerator. Sprinkle with salt and eat as is, or spread it on toast.

If you like creamy cottage cheese, like the kind we buy in stores today, stir in a tablespoon of cream before chilling your curds.

Porridge

Everyone ate porridge. It was made from any kind of grain: wheat, rye, or oats. Very poor people added lots of water to their porridge to make it go farther. Then it was called *gruel*.

Make some oatmeal porridge for yourself.

Spices were used to cover the taste of rotted or bland foods. They were so valuable that they were sometimes used instead of money. A pound of pepper cost 2 or 3 weeks of farm labor.

INGREDIENTS

⅓ cup oatmeal
¾ cup water
Milk
Brown sugar or honey
Raisins or other dried fruit (optional)

UTENSILS

Small pot
Cooking spoon

Heat the water in a small pot until it bubbles. Then stir in the oats. Bring the heat down to simmer, and let the oats cook for 5 minutes, stirring now and then. Let them sit for a minute to cool and thicken. Eat your porridge hot with milk and brown sugar or honey. Stir in raisins or other dried fruit while it's cooking, if you like.

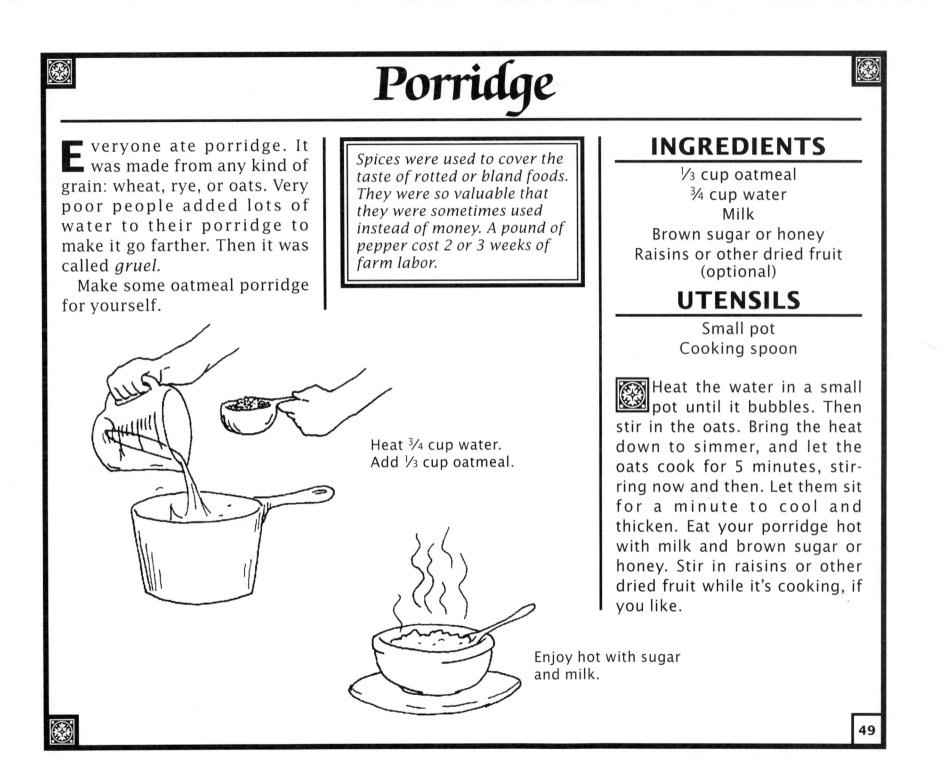

Heat ¾ cup water.
Add ⅓ cup oatmeal.

Enjoy hot with sugar and milk.

Cabbage Stew & Dumplings

INGREDIENTS

Stew
Small head of cabbage
3 carrots
¼ onion
2 leeks
6 cups water
6 beef bouillon cubes
½ teaspoon salt

Dumplings
½ cup flour
2 teaspoons baking powder
¾ teaspoon salt
3 tablespoons shortening
¾ cup milk

UTENSILS

Stew
Knife
Large pot with lid
Cooking spoon

Dumplings
Bowl
Mixing spoon
Fork

This makes a nice dinner for the whole family. If you've never tried dumplings, you may be surprised. In the Middle Ages most family meals were cooked in a large pot hung over a fire in the middle of the room. New things were added to the pot each day, and it was seldom emptied.

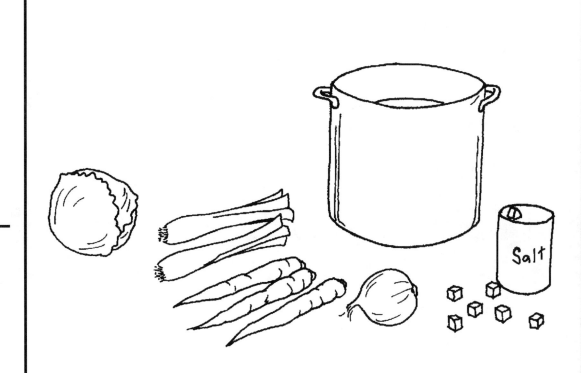

First, make the stew. If you've never seen a leek before, they look like big green onions. Wash, peel, and chop the vegetables into 1-inch pieces. Put everything in the pot and bring it to a boil. When the water begins to bubble, turn the heat down, cover the pot with the lid, and let it simmer for 15 minutes.

While the stew is cooking, you can make the dumplings.

Mix the flour, baking powder, and salt in the bowl. Add the shortening and mix it with the fork until the mixture is crumbly. Stir in the milk.

Divide the dough into 8 large lumps, and drop it into the stew. Let the dumplings cook for 10 minutes, then cover the pot with the lid and let it all cook 10 minutes more.

Serve it in a bowl or on a trencher.

To make tough, lean meat look better to shoppers, sneaky butchers sometimes cut a layer of fat from good meat and sewed it onto lean pieces.

Spoon the dumplings onto the stew while it cooks.

Pies & Tarts

Pie shells were called *coffins* and were filled with different kinds of meat and vegetables, or with fruit and custard. Use ready-made pie crusts, pie crust mixes, or this pastry recipe for the crusts.

This recipe makes one pie shell or 8 tarts.

Mix the flour, salt, and shortening using the fork. Mash it until it is completely mixed and becomes crumbly.

Add the water and form the mixture into a large ball of dough.

Sprinkle flour on the counter top and rolling pin to keep it from sticking. Make the rolling easy by laying a piece of plastic wrap over the dough and then rolling over it. Trim the dough with a knife so that it fits the pie pan. If you are making tarts, use a small bowl or empty coffee can to cut them out. Bake them in a cupcake pan.

Bake in a 450-degree oven for 9 minutes.

INGREDIENTS

1½ cups flour
½ teaspoon salt
½ cup shortening
4 tablespoons cold water

UTENSILS

Mixing bowl
Fork
Plastic wrap
Rolling pin
Knife, or small bowl or empty coffee can
Pie or cupcake pan

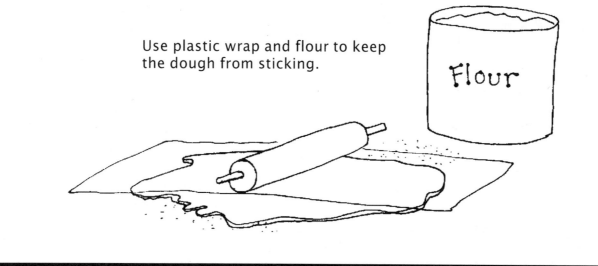

Use plastic wrap and flour to keep the dough from sticking.

Pocket Pies

INGREDIENTS

Tube of refrigerator biscuits

Filling:
canned cherry pie filling
or beef stew

Flour

UTENSILS

Rolling pin
Fork
Cookie sheet

 Sprinkle a few spoonfuls of flour on the counter top. Use the rolling pin to roll the biscuits flat. Spoon the cherries or stew onto the center of a biscuit. Don't put much juice or gravy on. Lay another flattened biscuit on top. Press the biscuits together around the edges with a fork. Prick the top with the fork to let steam escape during baking. Place the little pies on an ungreased cookie sheet and bake at 400° for 10 minutes.

Pies were eaten by everyone in the Middle Ages. You can make little pies filled with meat, vegetables, or fruit. Little pies like this are called *pasties* and were handy to eat when traveling or working in the field. Make some of your own for a picnic or school lunch.

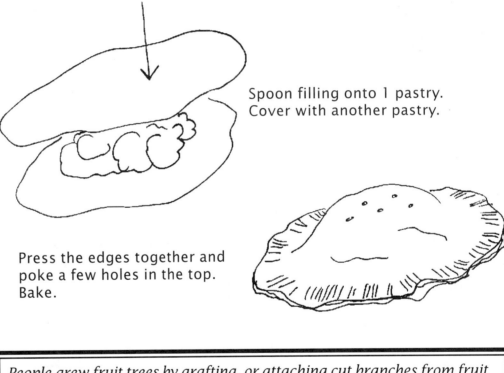

Spoon filling onto 1 pastry.
Cover with another pastry.

Press the edges together and poke a few holes in the top. Bake.

People grew fruit trees by grafting, or attaching cut branches from fruit trees to strong-growing oaks, and covering the cut edges with clay, moss, and cloth. Grafting improved the fruit trees, giving them better root systems.

Meat Pie

Fry the meat (ask an adult to help here). Lay 3 paper towels on a plate and spoon the cooked meat on top so that the fat and grease drain onto the towels.

Mix the eggs, milk, cooked meat, and a couple pinches of herbs in the bowl.

Pour the mixture into the pie shell and bake in a 350-degree oven for 35 minutes.

You can tell when it's done by sticking a knife in the center; if the knife comes out clean, it's ready.

Eat the pie while it's still warm—mmmm!

INGREDIENTS

Unbaked pie shell (with pie tin)

1 pound beef, pork sausage, or hamburger

3 eggs

½ cup milk

Herbs: sage, oregano, or thyme

UTENSILS

Frying pan
Large spoon
Plate
Paper towels
Mixing bowl

Meat had to be salted heavily to keep it from spoiling during the winter. Because salt cost a lot, only the best pieces were preserved. That's where we got the phrase, "Not worth his salt."

Raisin Custard Tarts

INGREDIENTS

Instant vanilla pudding

Milk
(amount according to
the pudding package)

½ cup raisins

6 baked tart shells

Jar with lid (mayonnaise-type)

Bake the tart shells. While the tart shells are cooling, prepare the pudding following package directions. Put the milk and pudding mix in the jar, fasten the lid, and shake to mix. Stir in the raisins.

Pour the pudding into the tart shells and let them chill in the refrigerator for a few minutes.

You can use a baked custard recipe here, but instant pudding is quicker and easier.

Milk

Instant Pudding

Raisins

4 & 20 Blackbird Pie

Some medieval cooks made a special pie that contained a very surprising filling. First, the cook baked a very large, empty pie crust. Then, he or she cut out a hole in the bottom crust and tucked several tiny, live birds inside the pie crust. The pie was cut open at the banquet and the guests were delighted when the birds fluttered out and around the hall. Another small pie was then served for eating.

Perhaps you've heard the rhyme about this unforgettable meal:

Sing a song of sixpence,
A pocket full of rye;
Four and twenty blackbirds
Baked in a pie;
When the pie was opened,
The birds began to sing;
Wasn't that a dainty dish
To set before the King?
You can't eat this blackbird pie, but it's fun to make.

Cut out the 24 blackbirds first. Fold the black paper in half twice. Cut along the folds to make 4 strips. Fold each strip in half once, and then fold it in thirds. (This way, you can cut 6 birds from each strip.) Trace or draw a bird shape and cut out through all sections at once. Be sure the head and tail are on the fold so that you don't cut through them. Fold and cut the other strips, making 24 birds. Tape the pieces together to make one long strip of birds. Fold them up accordion-style.

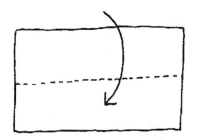

Fold the paper in half.

MATERIALS

9-by-11-inch sheet of black construction paper
6-by-6-inch sheet of tan construction paper
5-inch, disposable pie tin
Pencil
Scissors
Tape
Brown crayon
Glue

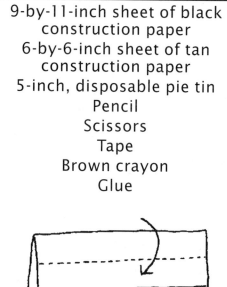

Fold it in half again.

Unfold and cut out 4 strips.

Cut out a small tab from the tan paper and tape it to the first bird's head.

Make the pie crust by tracing the pan rim on tan paper. Cut it out, making the edge sort of wavy, like a pie crust. Color bits of it with a brown crayon to make it look baked.

Cut a 2½-inch slit in the center of the crust. Trim the sides of the slit so it is about ¼ inch wide.

Glue the crust to the rim of the pie pan. When it's dry, carefully tuck the folded band of birds into the pie through the slit.

When you want the birds to come out of the pie, gently pull on the tab and the strip of birds will unfold as they "fly" out!

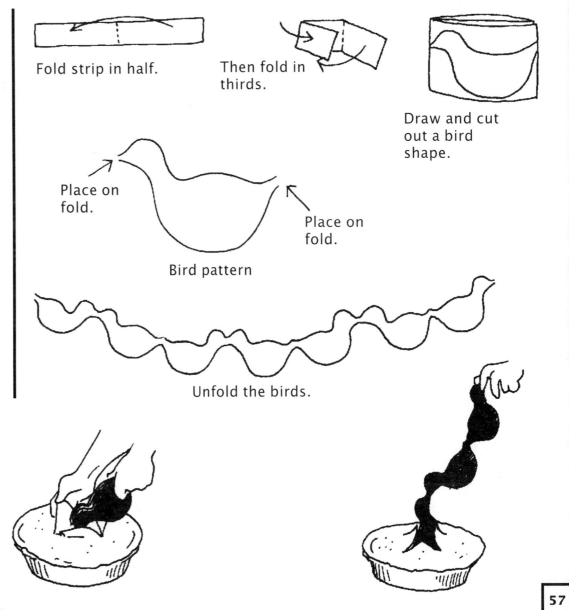

Fold strip in half.

Then fold in thirds.

Draw and cut out a bird shape.

Place on fold.

Place on fold.

Bird pattern

Unfold the birds.

Blackbird Pie Puppet

MATERIALS

Black construction paper
Tan construction paper
5-inch, disposable pie tin
Popsicle stick
Pencil
Scissors
Brown crayon
Glue

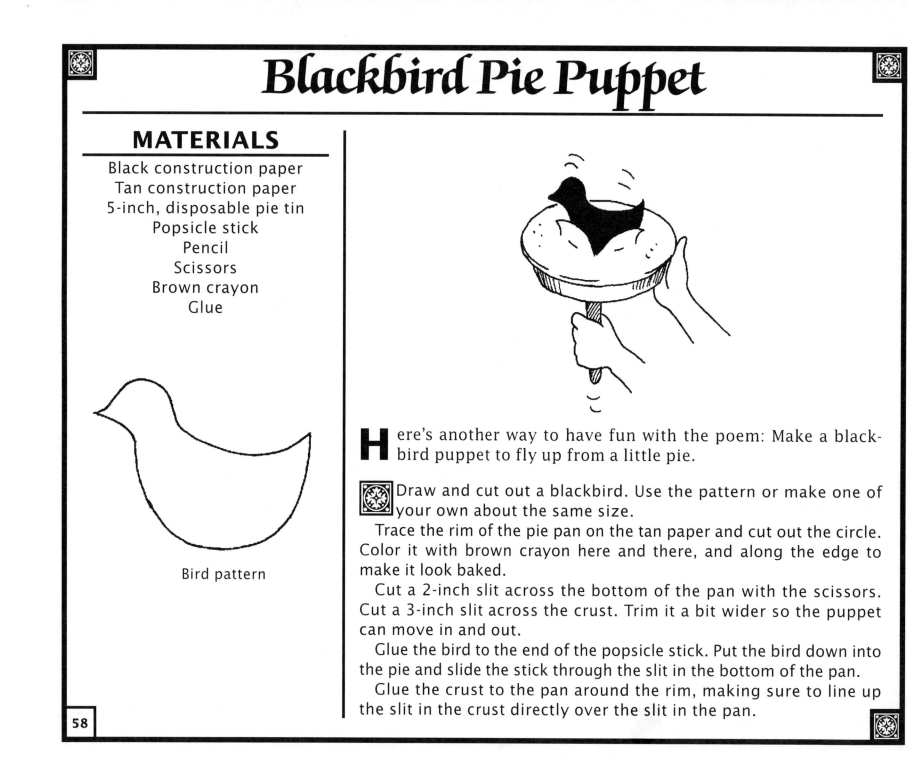

Bird pattern

Here's another way to have fun with the poem: Make a black-bird puppet to fly up from a little pie.

Draw and cut out a blackbird. Use the pattern or make one of your own about the same size.

Trace the rim of the pie pan on the tan paper and cut out the circle. Color it with brown crayon here and there, and along the edge to make it look baked.

Cut a 2-inch slit across the bottom of the pan with the scissors. Cut a 3-inch slit across the crust. Trim it a bit wider so the puppet can move in and out.

Glue the bird to the end of the popsicle stick. Put the bird down into the pie and slide the stick through the slit in the bottom of the pan.

Glue the crust to the pan around the rim, making sure to line up the slit in the crust directly over the slit in the pan.

Gingerbread Dolls

INGREDIENTS

½ cup sugar
½ cup shortening
½ cup dark molasses
¼ cup water
½ teaspoon salt
¾ teaspoon ground ginger
½ teaspoon cinnamon
½ teaspoon baking soda
2¾ cups flour

UTENSILS

Measuring cups and spoons
Mixing bowl
Mixing spoon
Plastic wrap
Rolling pin
Cookie cutters or a toothpick
and table knife
Cookie sheet

To make your own cookie cutter, cut both ends out of a clean, tuna fish can. Bend the can into a simple shape, and use it for cookies and biscuits.

Children looked forward to going to the fair, where small dolls made of spicy dough were sold. They could play with the dolls, and then eat them!

Here's a recipe for the gingerbread dolls they once enjoyed.

Preheat the oven to 375°. Mix together the sugar, shortening, molasses, and water. Add the rest of the ingredients. Mix until you have a nice stiff dough.

Sprinkle flour on the counter top and place the dough on it. Keep the rolling pin dusted with flour so that the dough won't stick to it. You can also place a large piece of plastic wrap between the dough and the rolling pin. Roll the dough flat, until it's as thick as a pancake (¼ inch).

Cut out the dough with gingerbread boy or girl cookie cutters. If you don't have any, draw an outline with a toothpick and cut around it with a knife. Be sure to make thick arms and legs or they will fall off.

Place the cutout cookies on an ungreased baking sheet and bake in the oven at 375° for 8 to 10 minutes.

Cut other shapes from gingerbread.

Make your own cookie cutter out of a tuna can.

Real Gingerbread

T his old recipe really is "gingered bread!" People long ago used every precious bit of food, creating tasty treats like this one from leftovers. Save dry bread slices until you have enough to make this.

If you don't have any dry bread, you can toast some a bit. Make small crumbs by putting the bread slices inside a plastic bread bag and crushing them with a rolling pin.

When you've crushed all the bread into fine crumbs, heat the honey in the saucepan until it starts bubbling (ask a grownup to help with the stove). Remove the pan from the heat and stir in the spices and crumbs. When it's all mixed, pack the mixture into a greased cake pan and press it down firmly. Let it harden for a few minutes. When it's firm, turn the pan upside down out onto a plate and slice the gingerbread into pieces with a knife.

Real gingerbread!

INGREDIENTS

Loaf of dried,
whole-wheat bread
½ cup honey
Teaspoon ground ginger
½ teaspoon cinnamon

UTENSILS

Rolling pin
Plastic bread bag
Saucepan
Cooking spoon
8-inch, greased cake pan
Plate
Knife

Crush the bread crumbs in a bag.

Real gingered bread!

Mead

INGREDIENTS

2 quarts cold water
½ to 1 cup honey
1 lemon or orange
Nutmeg
Ice cubes

UTENSILS

Pitcher
Stirring spoon
Knife

Add ½ cup of honey to the water in the pitcher, stirring to mix. Add more honey until it's as sweet as you want it.

Wash the lemon or orange and slice it in rounds. Add to the mead. Sprinkle on a bit of nutmeg.

Chill or serve with ice cubes.

In medieval days, spices were very costly. A pound of ginger was worth 1 sheep, a pound of nutmeg traded for 7 oxen.

Here's a sweet drink to go with your meal. In the Middle Ages, it was left to ferment a bit, but you can drink yours right away.

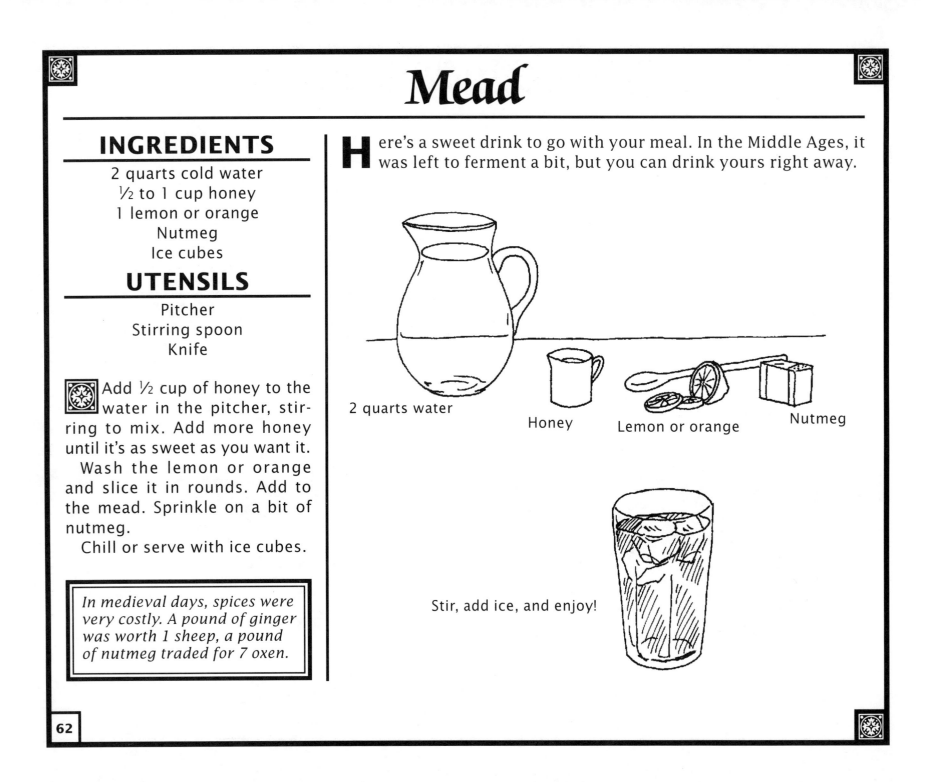

2 quarts water

Honey

Lemon or orange

Nutmeg

Stir, add ice, and enjoy!

Marvelous Marzipan

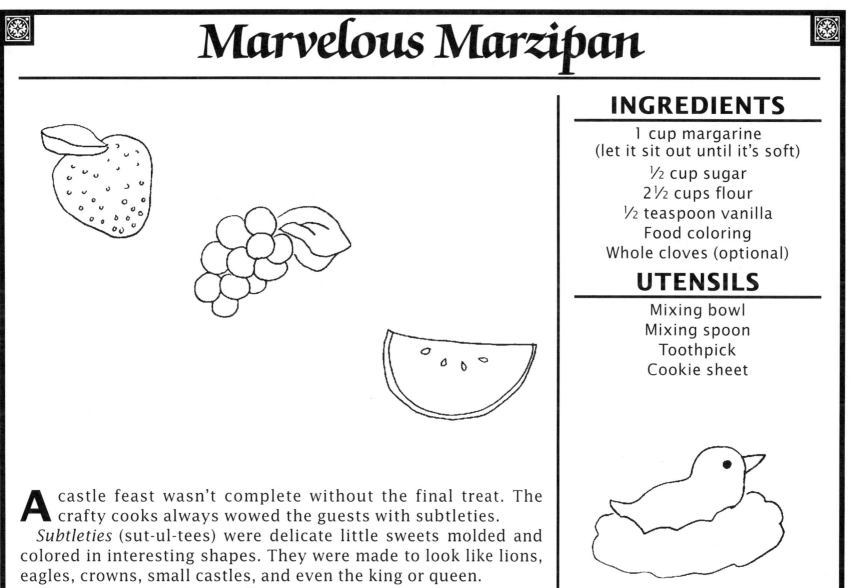

INGREDIENTS

1 cup margarine
(let it sit out until it's soft)
½ cup sugar
2½ cups flour
½ teaspoon vanilla
Food coloring
Whole cloves (optional)

UTENSILS

Mixing bowl
Mixing spoon
Toothpick
Cookie sheet

A castle feast wasn't complete without the final treat. The crafty cooks always wowed the guests with subtleties.

Subtleties (sut-ul-tees) were delicate little sweets molded and colored in interesting shapes. They were made to look like lions, eagles, crowns, small castles, and even the king or queen.

They were made from jellies, pastry, or ground nuts. Sugar wasn't used at that time. Honey was used for sweetening instead.

The clever subtleties were shown off to the admiring guests, then eaten.

Mix the margarine and sugar together. Stir in the flour and vanilla. It will be crumbly.

Divide the dough into parts, one for each color you want to use. Add one drop of color at a time to the dough, until it's the color you want.

Shape the dough into fruits, vegetables, tiny dolls, or castles. Try a bird in a nest or a frog on a lily pad. You can add details using a toothpick, use whole cloves for flower stems or eyes. Use your imagination—that's what the King's cooks did! Put your creations on an ungreased cookie sheet and chill in the refrigerator for half an hour.

Preheat the oven to 300°, and bake your subtleties 30 minutes, or until baked but not browned.

Make castles and crowns you can eat!

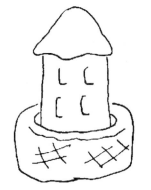

Heraldry

In the Middle Ages, people were very interested in knowing about their ancestors and in showing other people what family they belonged to. They kept records about their family history and passed them onto the next generation.

People made up family designs, or *crests,* that were passed down, too. These designs were an important way to show the family line that you were a part of. They also made everyday life more colorful.

Your Coat of Arms

Come up with your own design and put it on flags, banners, shields, clothing, jewelry, and writing paper.

Trace the basic shape in the illustration. Start designing your coat of arms with simple lines and two colors, one dark and one light. Use red, blue, black, green, or purple. Medieval people used gold and silver, too, but yellow and white will do. Only bright colors—no pastels—were used.

Once you decide on your basic design, add simple things like birds, beasts, and monsters, if you like. Lions, eagles, and dragons were symbols of strength. Flowers, such as roses, or thistles and trees were popular, too. Use your imagination and some bright colors to create a crest for yourself or your family. Put it on things you make or wear.

Some simple designs

Here are some designs that were popular.

Mini-Banner

MATERIALS

Brightly colored felt
Yarn, about 24 inches
Pencil
Paper
Scissors
Glue

Cloth banners were used to decorate the walls inside the castle. Knights also carried them to show what family they belonged to. Make a simple banner to hang on your wall or to decorate a Christmas tree.

Plan your design with paper and pencil first. Cut out a banner shape in the felt. Glue on small pieces of different-colored felt. Leave some space on the edge of the banner.

Lay the yarn across the top edge of the banner. Fold the edge over the yarn and glue the edge down.

Tie the ends of the yarn together in a knot and hang it from a nail or thumbtack.

You can make very large banners for your room or a festival by using colored butcher paper with a strip of cardboard inside the fold to hold the shape.

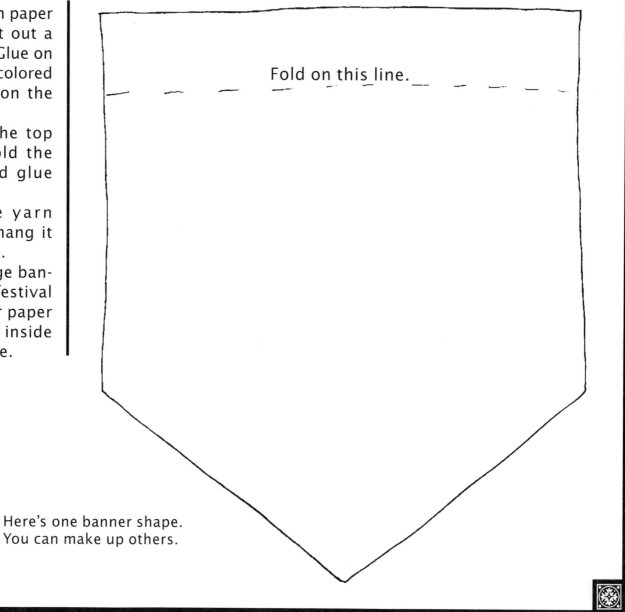

Fold on this line.

Here's one banner shape.
You can make up others.

Family Names

Family names, or last names, have only been used for about 900 years. Before that time, people lived in small communities where everyone knew each other. One name was all anyone needed. As the number of people grew larger and things like travel and trade brought strangers together, a second name began to be used. The second name was important because it showed what family a person belonged to.

Some of the last names came from the parent's name: Carl's Son became Carlson; Erik's Son became Erikson. Or, names came from a person's job: the miller's family became the Millers; the sheepherder's family became the Shepherds.

Many last names came from words describing where the person lived, such as Atwood, Atwater, Lane, Woods, and Rivers.

Last names were passed on to children and their children, and became a symbol of the family and what it stood for. People took pride in the tradition and successes of their ancestors.

Families were very important in the Middle Ages. Relatives did business with one another, protected and fought for each other, arranged marriages for their children, and passed down land and wealth.

A family name was something to take pride in, and protecting your "good name" was very important.

Think about your family's last name. Did it come from the Middle Ages? Ask your parents and grandparents to help you look it up in *genealogy* (family history) books at the library.

King Edward V passed a law to make Irish people use last names. It said: "They shall take a last name, of some town, or color (like Black or Brown), or some art (like Smith or Carpenter), or some job (like Cooke or Butler)." The same law was passed for Jewish people in Germany and Austria.

Your Family Tree

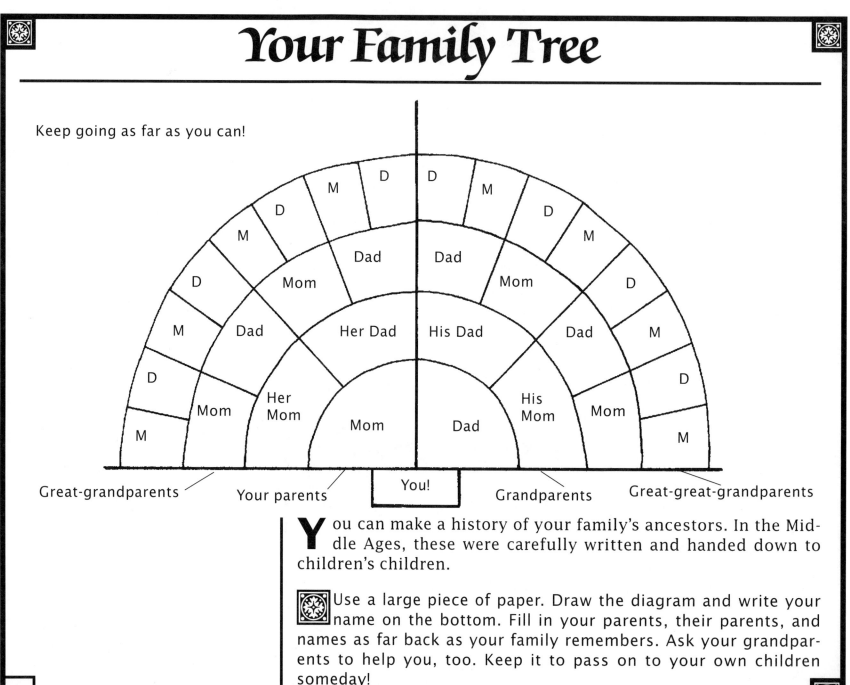

Keep going as far as you can!

Great-grandparents   Your parents   You!   Grandparents   Great-great-grandparents

You can make a history of your family's ancestors. In the Middle Ages, these were carefully written and handed down to children's children.

Use a large piece of paper. Draw the diagram and write your name on the bottom. Fill in your parents, their parents, and names as far back as your family remembers. Ask your grandparents to help you, too. Keep it to pass on to your own children someday!

Life Mask

MATERIALS

Plaster bandages
(from a drugstore)

Petroleum jelly
(like Vaseline brand)

Plastic wrap
Bowl of water
Paint
Wire
Clips or headband
Old shirt
Scissors
Hole punch
Paper towels for cleanup

Death masks of relatives were hung on walls to remind everyone that the family was part of a longer family line.

Cover the face with Vaseline and 2 strips of plastic wrap.

In the Middle Ages, wealthy people had an unusual way of remembering a dead loved one's face—death masks. Since there were no photographs in those days and very few artists painted portraits, this was a good way to show what they had looked like.

You can make a mask of yourself, with lots of help from a friend. The person being "masked" must be ready to sit still for about half an hour while the mask is being put on, and while it hardens.

Make sure that a grown-up helps you with this project. Pick a friend whose face you'd like to remember forever. Pull your friend's hair back with clips or a headband. Cover his or her face with a coating of Vaseline so the plaster won't dry on the skin. Put a piece of plastic wrap across the closed eyelids so that nothing will get in the subject's eyes. Put another strip across the mouth area. Don't put anything over the nostrils, just Vaseline around them.

Tear or cut the bandages in short strips. Wet them in the water and lay them across the face. Smooth them down gently with your fingers and lay another layer on top. Be sure to leave the nostrils open for breathing.

When the face is covered, wait a few minutes for the plaster to harden. Gently pull the edges of the mask away from the face. Once the mask is off of the person's face, put plaster bandages over the nose area of the mask.

When it's completely dry, paint your mask; gold is a good color. Punch holes in the corners and hang it from the wall with a wire.

Layer on the wet bandages. Leave the nose open.

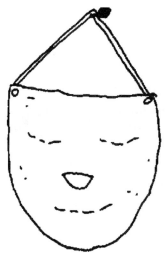

Hang it on the wall.

Fun & Games

Everyone—young and old, rich and poor—played games in the Middle Ages. They made up many different games and played them indoors and out. Some games were created to practice strategy for warfare, such as chess and other games where playing pieces were "captured." Dice games that involved gambling were also popular. Sometimes players would gamble on the outcome of a game, putting up jewelry, coins, or other possessions. Other games were just for fun and were played during people's spare time or at the great fairs. Many of the games we play today were first made up by fun-loving people during the Middle Ages.

Most people owned game pieces made of wood or stones. Wealthy people had their game pieces made from gold, precious stones, or ivory. You can use materials you have around the house to make games like people did centuries ago.

Alquerque

*A*lquerque (say it: all-kwair-kay) is one of the first board games ever created. It was played in ancient Egypt and was brought to Europe by the Arabs. Today we play checkers or *draughts,* which was created from it. This game is for 2 players.

MATERIALS

Paper or tagboard,
4 by 4 inches
24 game pieces
(12 for each player):
pennies and nickels or
2 colors of cutout tagboard
Pencil
Ruler
Marker

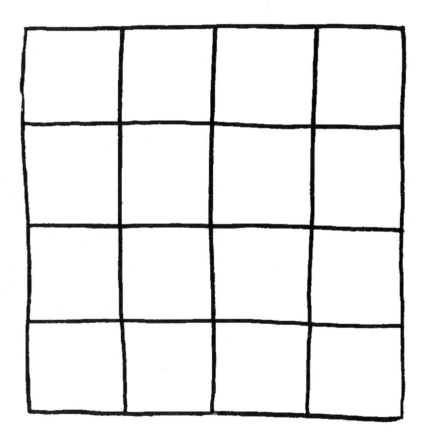

Draw the squares on the game board with a pencil and ruler. Cut out or find game pieces.

To play: Set up the pieces as shown. Take turns moving the game pieces from corner to corner diagonally. If your piece moves onto one that already holds the other player's game piece, you can "capture" it, take it off the board, and put your own game piece on that spot.

After your game piece reaches the opposite edge of the board, it can then move both forwards and backwards along the straight lines as well as the diagonals.

The winner is the last one with game pieces left on the board.

Chess was a very popular game. It gave knights a chance to practice situations they might face in war.

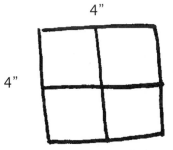

Make a box and draw a cross in it.

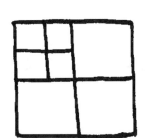

Put a cross in the 4 boxes.

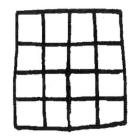

Done!

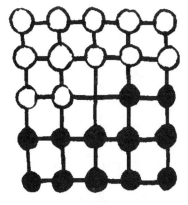

Set up the pieces like this. Go ahead—it's your move!

Draughts

MATERIALS

Paper or tagboard,
8 by 8 inches

24 game pieces
(12 pieces for each player):
buttons, plastic lids,
cutout cardboard or
styrofoam, or
self-hardening clay

Pencil

Ruler

2 colors of markers or paint

Draughts (say it: "drafts") is the game we now play called checkers. It was once called *ferses,* too. Make yourself a set of handmade pieces and a game board. This game is for 2 players.

Use the ruler to mark the halfway point of the square, then mark these 2 sections in half, and each of these sections in half. That makes 8 sections. Do the same thing going the other direction, and you will have 64 squares on the board. Use the markers to color every other square the same color.

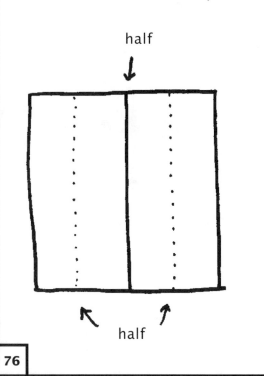

half

half

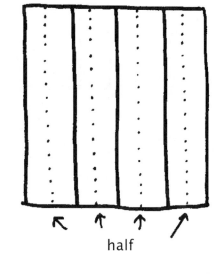

half

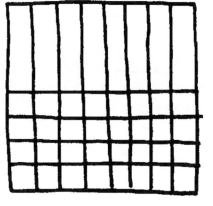

Do the same going the opposite direction.

To play: Each player lines up the game pieces on the dark squares on their side of the board. Take turns moving them across the board, moving diagonally only. Jump other players if they sit next to yours, and take them off the board. When your pieces reach the last row on the other side they are "King-ed"—topped with a piece. This means that they can move in any direction. The last player with pieces on the board wins.

In France, the first players of this game used the rule that you didn't *have* to jump a game piece if another move was possible.

Color every other square
to make a pattern.

Fox & Geese

This game came from the Vikings of Scandinavia and Iceland. It's for 2 players.

Draw the game board like the one in the illustration. Put the game pieces on the spots as shown.

To play: The pennies are geese and the dime is the fox. One person moves the fox along the lines in any direction. The other player moves the geese along the lines in any direction. The fox can jump the geese and then they are taken off the board. The geese cannot jump. The object of the game is for the geese to try to get in position so that the fox can't move in any direction.

MATERIALS
Paper or tagboard,
6 by 6 inches
Game pieces:
13 pennies and 1 dime
Pencil
Ruler
Marker

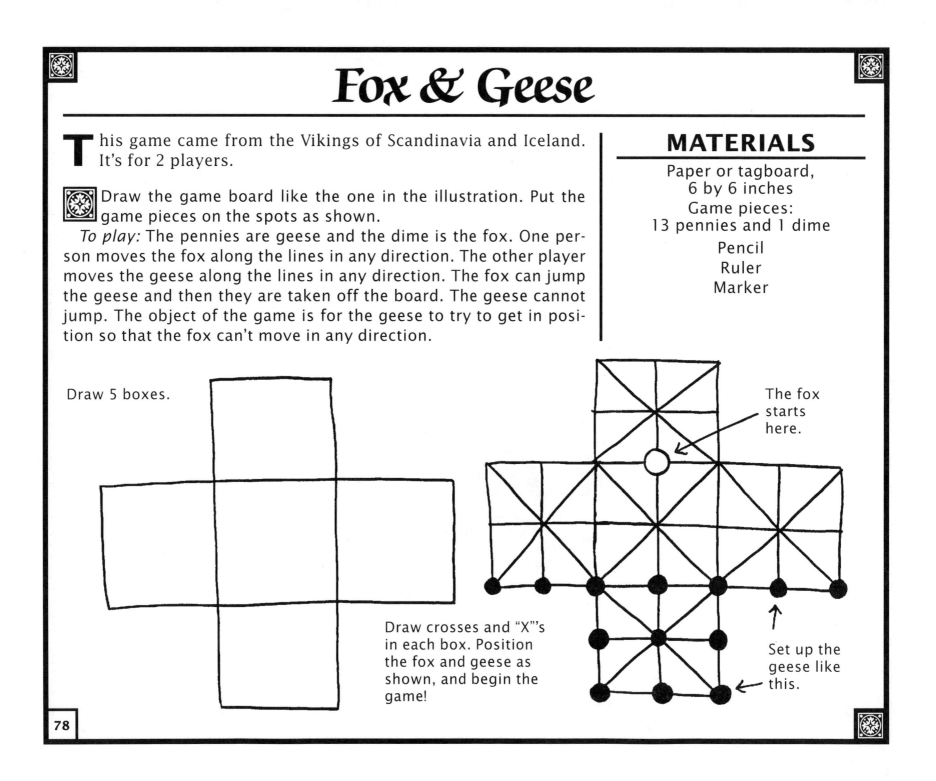

Draw 5 boxes.

Draw crosses and "X"'s in each box. Position the fox and geese as shown, and begin the game!

The fox starts here.

Set up the geese like this.

Three Throws

MATERIALS

Milk or juice cartons, or paper
Colored paper or paint
Scissors
Glue

Use clean milk or juice cartons to make a giant set. Cut and tape a small milk carton to make a cube. Glue colored paper to the outside, or paint it.

Many games using dice were popular in the Middle Ages. You can make some for yourself, and then play this game. It's very simple, and any number of people can play. Use one, two, or even three dice—whatever you want.

Cut out flaps and tape them down to make a box.

Open up the top of the carton.

Add dots.

MILK-CARTON DICE

If you want to make a small set of paper dice, trace the pattern onto your paper as shown. Add flaps for folding and gluing. Write numbers or draw dots in each square using numbers between 1 and 6. Cut it out on the solid lines. Fold the flaps in and fold along all lines to shape into a cube. Glue the flaps to the inside.

To play: Each person tosses the dice 3 times. Add the number of points for each toss to get a total score. The winner is the one with the highest score after 1 round.

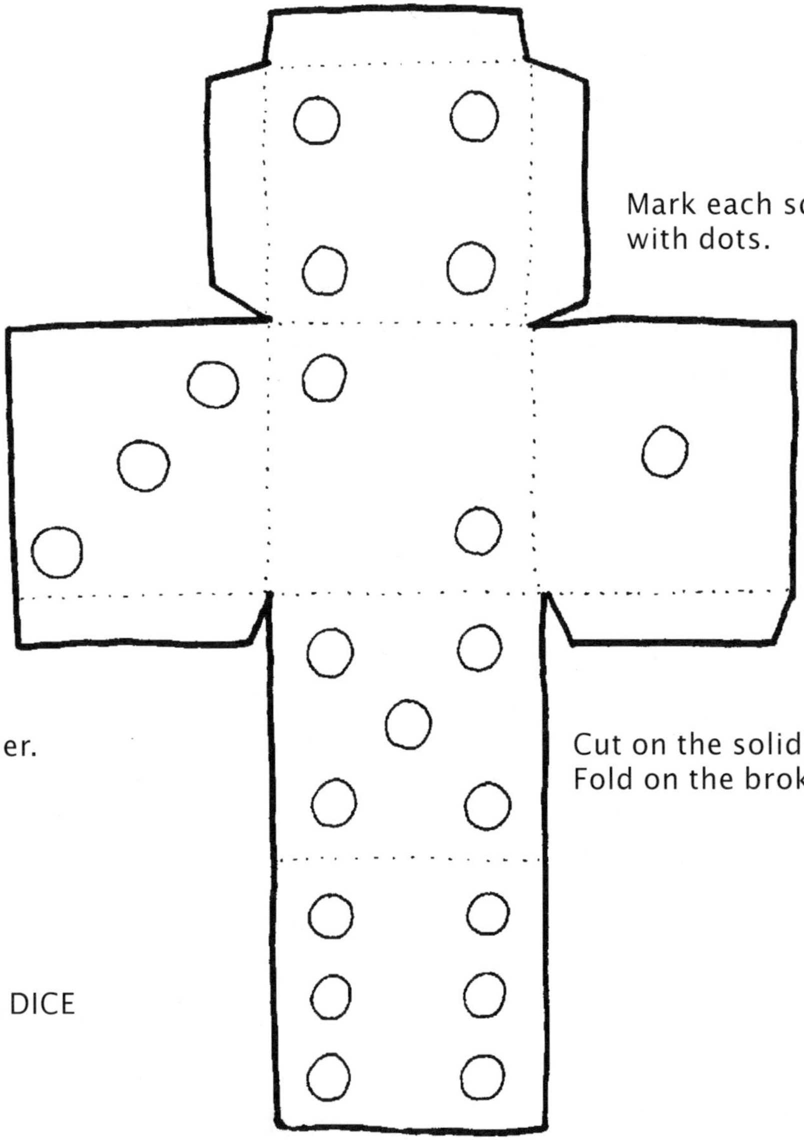

Mark each square with dots.

Fold and glue together.

Cut on the solid lines.
Fold on the broken lines.

PAPER DICE

Goose

MATERIALS

Paper or cardboard
Place markers
(1 for each player):
pebbles, coins, buttons, paper
clips, or bottle caps
Die
Colored markers

This game came from 14th-century Italy. Many board games today are based on it. Two to ten people can play.

Draw a spiral race track on the paper. Draw a goose on every fifth space.

To play: Start on the outside of the spiral. Take turns rolling the die. Move your markers the number of spaces shown on the die. If you land on a goose, you get another roll of the die. Keep rolling the die and moving your markers toward the center. To win, you must roll the exact number needed to end at the center spot. The first player to get to the center wins.

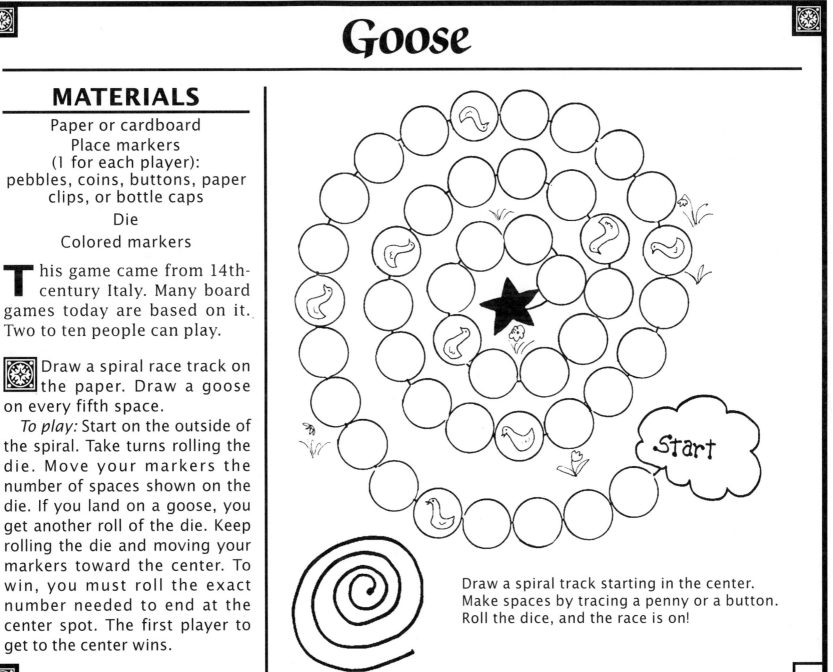

Draw a spiral track starting in the center. Make spaces by tracing a penny or a button. Roll the dice, and the race is on!

9 Men's Morris

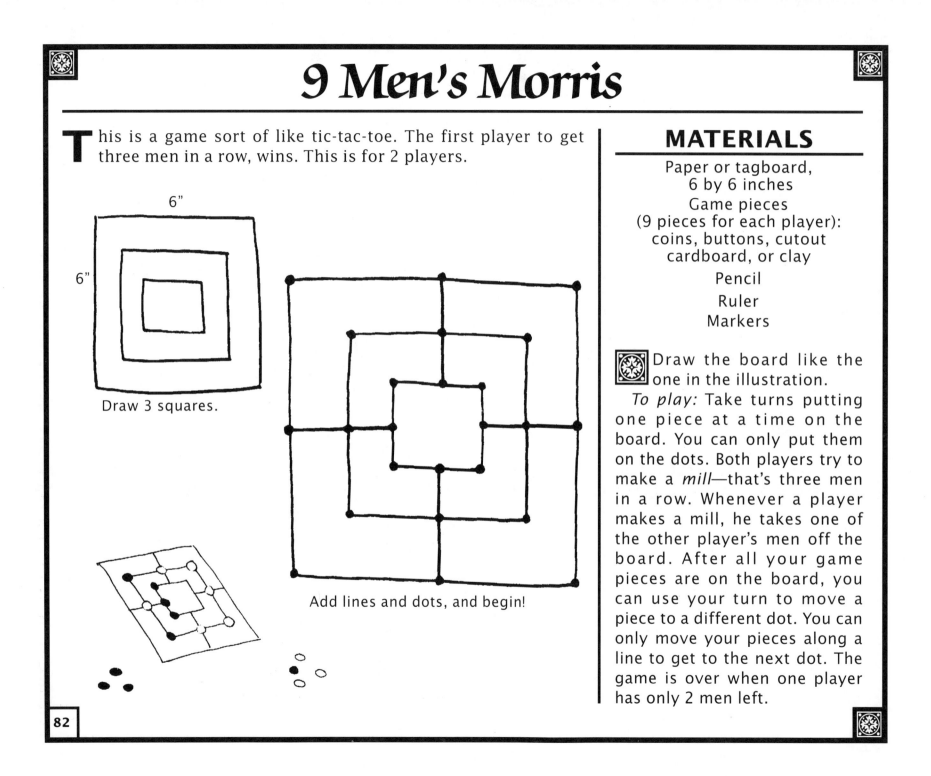

This is a game sort of like tic-tac-toe. The first player to get three men in a row, wins. This is for 2 players.

6"

6"

Draw 3 squares.

Add lines and dots, and begin!

MATERIALS

Paper or tagboard,
6 by 6 inches
Game pieces
(9 pieces for each player):
coins, buttons, cutout
cardboard, or clay
Pencil
Ruler
Markers

Draw the board like the one in the illustration.

To play: Take turns putting one piece at a time on the board. You can only put them on the dots. Both players try to make a *mill*—that's three men in a row. Whenever a player makes a mill, he takes one of the other player's men off the board. After all your game pieces are on the board, you can use your turn to move a piece to a different dot. You can only move your pieces along a line to get to the next dot. The game is over when one player has only 2 men left.

Gluckshaus

MATERIALS

Paper or tagboard,
6 by 7 inches

Dried beans

Dice (see p. 79 to make some)

Pencil

Ruler

Colored markers

Copy the board design. Put the numbers in the same spaces. Use markers to draw pictures for the King, Wedding, and Lucky Pig spaces. Real Gluckshaus boards were made from beautifully painted wood. Draw and decorate yours however you like, but be sure you have the three pictures in the proper places.

*G*luckshaus means "house of fortune," and if you want to win this German game, all you need is luck. Today's game of roulette came from it. Any number of players can play.

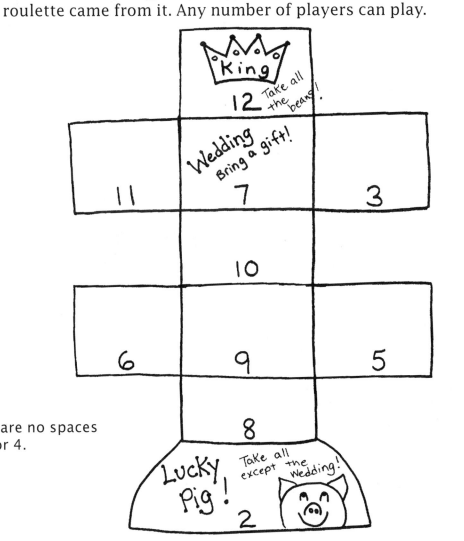

There are no spaces for 1 or 4.

To play: Give each player 10 beans (you can give more—any amount is fine). The players take turns tossing two dice. Then they put 1 bean on the square of the number they rolled on the dice. If a bean is already in the square, they take it, instead of leaving one.

Beans can't be taken from the Wedding space—because you always take a gift to a wedding. If you roll a 2, the Lucky Pig, you get to take all the beans on the board, except the ones on the Wedding space. If you roll a 12, the King, you get *all* the beans on the board. This is the only time you may take the beans in the Wedding space.

Keep rolling the dice, and putting or taking beans, until only one player is left with beans.

In 15th-century German social clubs, it was against the rules to go barefoot, roll in the mud, steal food, or throw knives and dishes.

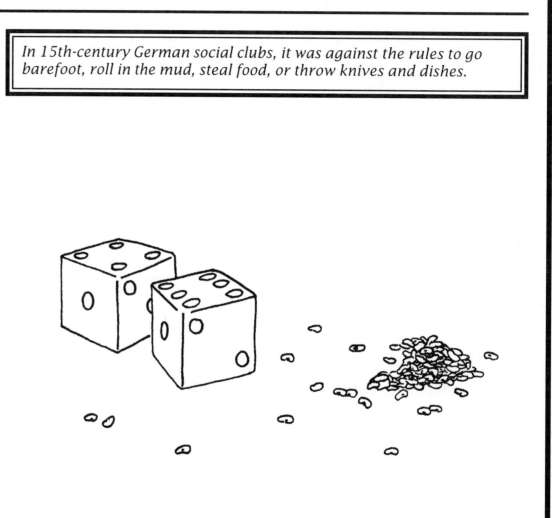

Blind Man's Bluff

This was called Hoodman's Blind in the Middle Ages because the blind player wore a hooded cape backwards over the face, instead of a blindfold.

To play, all you need is cloth for a blindfold and a group of friends.

One person is blindfolded and the other players form a circle around him or her. A player gently taps the blindfolded player. Without peeking, the blindfolded player guesses who did the tapping. If he or she guesses right, the blindfolded player switches places with the person who tapped. If not, others take turns tapping.

Shoebox Psaltery

A *psaltery* (say it: sall-turry) was a musical instrument played at banquets or for the royal court in the castle.

Wrap rubber bands around a shoebox.

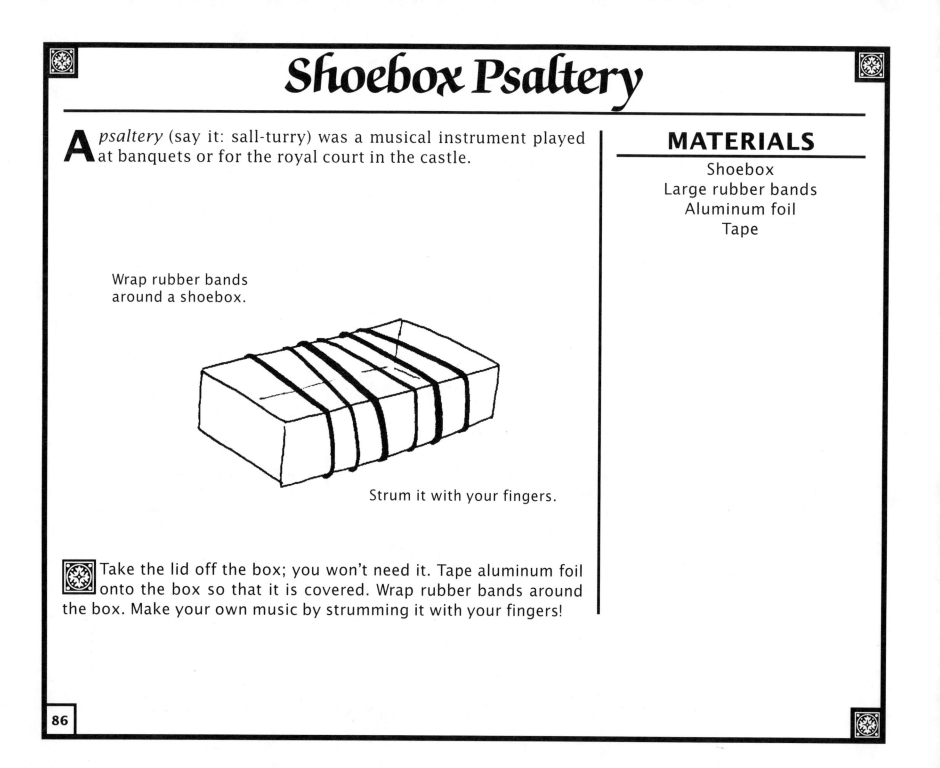

Strum it with your fingers.

Take the lid off the box; you won't need it. Tape aluminum foil onto the box so that it is covered. Wrap rubber bands around the box. Make your own music by strumming it with your fingers!

Puppets

3-by-5-inch index cards or
any stiff paper
Penny or dime
Pencil
Crayons or markers
Scissors

People traveled long distances to attend the Great Fairs. They were held once a year in the towns. Traders, merchants, entertainers, and craftspeople came to trade or entertain everyone. The fairs grew larger every year as more people began to enjoy traveling and trading. People liked seeing new things, such as firecrackers from far-off China and potatoes from the New World.

Between visiting and trading, people enjoyed watching entertainment by jugglers, minstrels, dancers, and puppeteers. Loud and lively puppet shows were very popular with adults and children, and they were always part of the fair. They especially liked shows that made them laugh.

Finger Puppets

Trace a penny or a dime, depending upon the size of your fingers, at one end of the index card. Cut out the circles. When you are happy with the fit, begin drawing and coloring your puppet on the rest of the card. Color it and cut out along the outer edges.

Make one for each hand, and let the show begin!

To cut out the finger holes,
fold the card over and snip the hole.
Then insert the scissors and cut.

MATERIALS

Tan fabric, 15 by 15 inches
(or a handkerchief)

3-inch ball or stuffing

Yarn

2 small pebbles

Scissors

Black and brown
fine-tipped markers

Pink crayon

Easy Marionette

Puppets held on strings were called *marionettes*. People liked them because they could be made to move so easily.

Place the ball on the upper part of the cloth.

Back view

Bring the puppet to life!

Put the ball in the upper middle of the cloth. Wrap it up and tie tightly with a short piece of yarn. Cut a 24-inch piece of yarn. With this piece of yarn, tie a pebble inside the upper corner of the cloth to make a hand. Do the same on the other corner with the other end of the yarn piece. Now you have arms and a loop to move them with.

With scissors, snip 2 tiny slits at the top back of the head. Thread a 20-inch piece of yarn through the slits and knot the ends. Now you have a loop to hold the head up with.

Use markers to draw on a face, and crayon to shade some cheek color.

Use the puppet as it is or make it some clothing from scraps. An aluminum foil crown, macaroni beads, yarn hair and a flowery cape—you've made a king or queen!

Dolls

Dolls in the Middle Ages were very simple. They were made of wood or cloth. Dollmakers sold dolls at the Great Fairs. As the years went by, they began to experiment and used papier mâché, sawdust, flour, and glue to make dolls. Children of royalty and wealth had many fine dolls; poor children had few. A poor child might have only had a doll made from a soup bone wrapped in a rag.

Boys played with small tin or wooden soldiers, too.

Queens and princesses bought dolls dressed in the latest fashions from far-off lands. Then their dressmakers could copy the stylish clothing for them. That's how they kept up with the latest fashions.

MATERIALS

Wooden clothespins
(without metal springs)

Fabric, thread, and paper scraps

Aluminum foil

Yarn

Modeling clay

Fine-tipped markers

Scissors

Glue

Wooden Dolls & Soldiers

Draw faces with markers on the ends of the clothespins, and then dress them with the scraps. Their clothing can be very simple. Use some of the clothing ideas in the illustration, or make up your own.

To make the people stand up, roll modeling clay into a small ball and press the clothespin "feet" firmly into it.

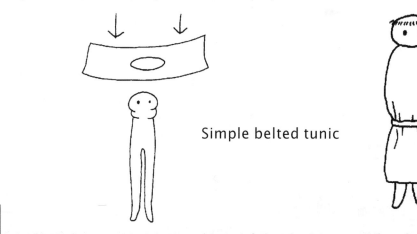

Simple belted tunic

Half-circle cape

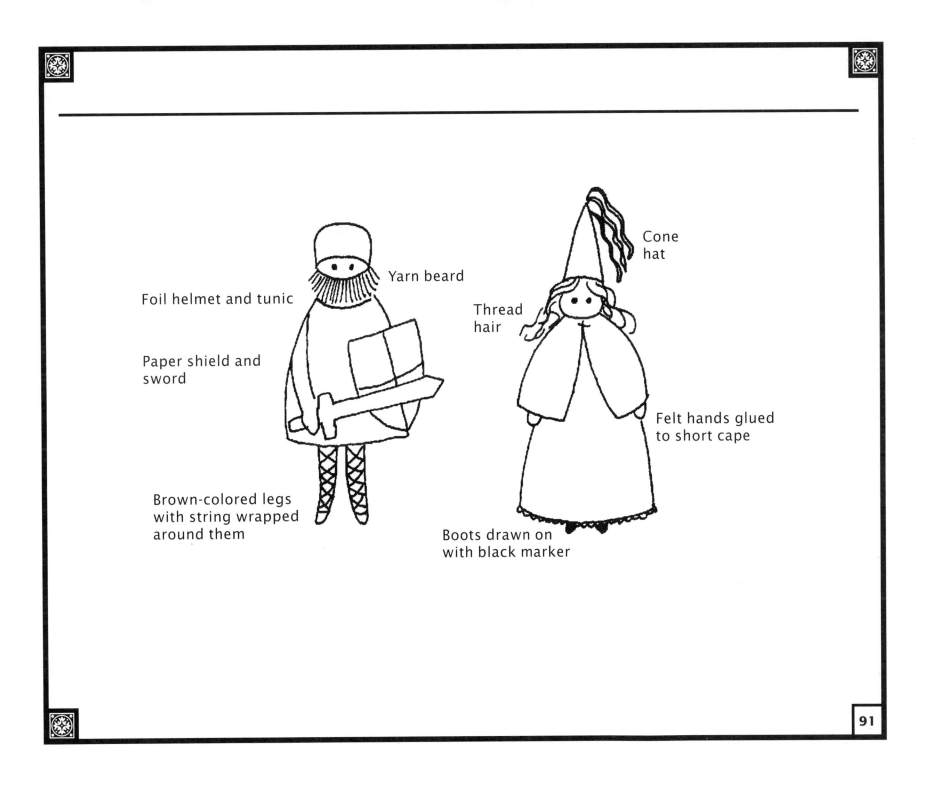

Foil helmet and tunic

Yarn beard

Paper shield and
sword

Brown-colored legs
with string wrapped
around them

Cone
hat

Thread
hair

Felt hands glued
to short cape

Boots drawn on
with black marker

MATERIALS

Yarn

Cardboard,
3 by 5 inches or larger

Dryer lint or stuffing

Fabric scraps

Scissors

Wind yarn around the cardboard.

Tie at 1 end.

Divide and tie at the other end.

Yarn Doll

Children probably made these with wool yarn from the family's sheep.

 Wind the yarn around the cardboard about 50 times. More yarn will make a fatter doll; less will make a thinner one.

Tie and knot a short piece of yarn through all the loops on one end. Divide the loops in two equal groups at the other end. Tie and knot lengths of yarn tightly around both groups.

Gently slip the loops off the cardboard.

Wad up some dryer lint or stuffing and push it inside the top part to fill out a head. Hide it with the yarn pieces. Knot a small piece of yarn underneath it for a neck.

Wind about 25 yarn loops around the cardboard and tie the ends to make arms. Slip it off the cardboard. Slide the arms into the body under the neck. Tie pieces of yarn across to hold the arms in place. Tie a waist, too. That's it!

Make simple clothes from felt or cloth scraps, if you wish.

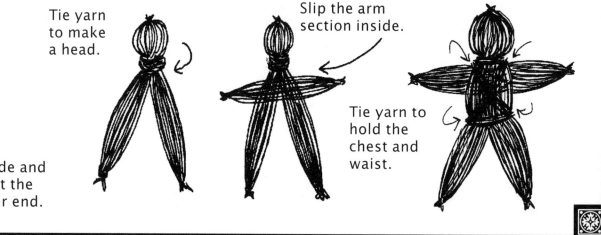

Tie yarn to make a head.

Slip the arm section inside.

Tie yarn to hold the chest and waist.

Sock Doll

 Cut off half of the cuff part of the sock. Cut the piece in half, turn inside out, and stitch to create arms. Turn right side out and stuff each arm lightly.

Cut the remaining cuff on the sock down the center, creating two leg sections. Turn the sock inside out and stitch the cut edges together for the legs. Stitch across the bottom of each.

Cut an opening at the toe end about 2 inches long, and turn the sock right side out through that opening. Stuff. Fill the rest of the body with stuffing, too. Don't stuff it too much or it will be too fat; it should be soft and floppy.

Turn the ends of the arms inside and sew them to the body with a needle and thread. Stitch the opening at the toe closed. Wrap and tie yarn or thread several times around the body above the arms. Pull the thread tight and knot to create a neck.

Stitch buttons for eyes, or embroider them. You can use fine-tipped markers or fabric paints. Freckles can be made with light brown colored pencil or marker. Rub a bit of red or pink crayon on the cheeks for blush. Make hair from yarn or strips of cloth.

MATERIALS
Old socks
Stuffing
(try cut-up nylon stockings)
Buttons
Yarn or cloth torn into strips
Needle and thread
Scissors
Fine-tipped markers, fabric paint, or embroidery thread
Crayons
Colored pencils or markers

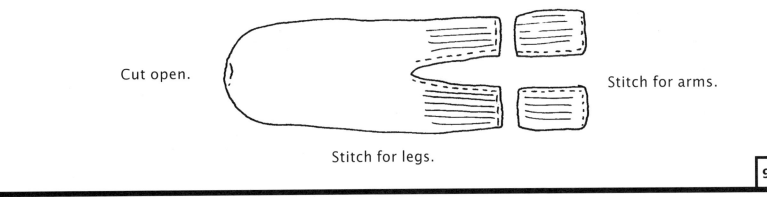

Cut open.

Stitch for arms.

Stitch for legs.

93

To make hair, cut 6-inch lengths of yarn and sew them in place with hand stitches down the center and back of the head. Trim the yarn evenly when you are finished.

The easiest way to cover your doll's head is with a cap. Just use another sock to make a cute little cap that fits your doll's head snugly. Cut away the cuff section of a sock. Pull the cut end together tightly and stitch securely with needle and thread. Turn right side out and put on the doll's head, turning it up to make a brim around the face.

For a baby doll, stitch a cap from a sock cuff, and wrap the baby in tiny cloth blanket.

Stitch yarn to typing paper for a wig. Pull the paper away.

Doll House

MATERIALS

Cardboard,
two 12-by-6-inch pieces and
one 12-inch circle

Small boxes, spools,
and container caps

Fabric and paper scraps

Serrated knife

Glue

 Cut two slits in the middle of the cardboard pieces like the drawing. Slide the pieces together at the slits. These are the walls for a 4-room cottage. Glue it to the round piece of cardboard and you're ready to decorate! Use scraps of felt, cloth, colored paper and trims.

Make furniture from small boxes, spools, and caps.

Peasant cottages had a room for the cow and chickens, too. You might want to decorate yours like that!

Adults and children enjoyed doll houses decorated with lots of tiny furniture. Make a little family of dolls from clay, paper, or clothespins (see p. 90). Then make this simple little house for them.

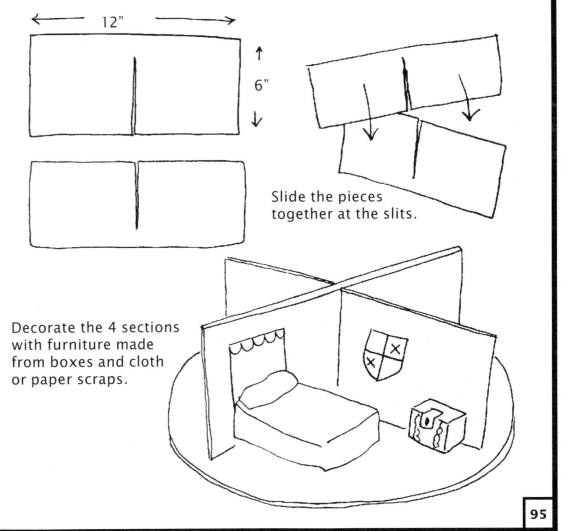

Slide the pieces together at the slits.

Decorate the 4 sections with furniture made from boxes and cloth or paper scraps.

Paper-Bag Prancer

You can make your own horse to ride in a tournament.

Cut open the 2 large bags and cut away the bottoms. Lay one flat. Begin at one end and roll it up tightly. Tape it in place. Lay down the other bag flat and roll it up over the tube, gluing and taping to hold. You can use only one sack for this, but two make the tube stronger.

Crush a sheet or two of old newspaper and gently stuff one of the small sacks. Fold the ends closed and staple to the paper tube.

Cut the bottom off the other small sack. Make a fringe out of it by cutting narrow strips, leaving about 1 inch uncut on one side. Staple it in place over the top and side of the horse's head. Gently crush the fringe with your hands to create a fluffy mane. Make some paper ears, too.

Decorate the pony's face with markers and you're ready to ride!

MATERIALS

2 lunch-sized brown paper bags
2 large brown paper bags
Newspaper
Tape
Glue
Stapler
Scissors
Markers

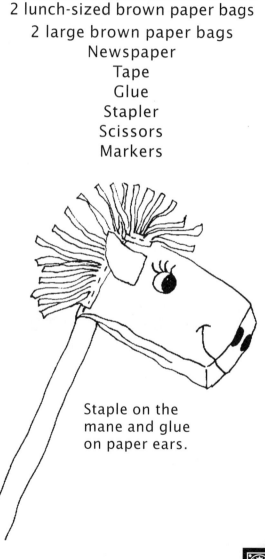

Staple on the mane and glue on paper ears.

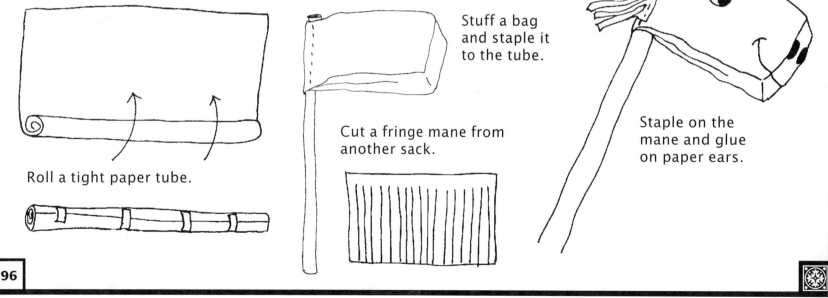

Roll a tight paper tube.

Cut a fringe mane from another sack.

Stuff a bag and staple it to the tube.

96

Juggling

MATERIALS

3 small balls
(or make them by
rolling up 3 socks)

Start with just one ball. Stand with your arms at your sides, hands held out and in front of you, with the palms facing up. Relax. Toss the ball from one hand to the other. Throw it up to arc over and fall into the other cupped hand.

When you can catch one ball easily, add a second ball and toss one up and the other across. This will take a bit of practice.

If you're able to juggle 2 balls, add another and toss 3 at once. Practice slowly—this isn't easy to do without concentration and hard work.

Try juggling colorful scarves, too. They are easy to catch because they fall slowly, and they are graceful to watch, too.

1 ball

2 balls

3 balls

Jugglers traveled to the Great Fairs to entertain everyone. They also performed for the knights and ladies in the castles after fancy banquets.

They wore bright colors. Points were cut along the edges of jugglers' clothing and tiny bells were sewn at the tips of them. Their fancy costumes made the jugglers exciting to watch and listen to.

Make Some Magic

Magicians, acrobats, and jugglers performed at the medieval banquets in the castles. Tight-rope walkers and stilt-walkers also entertained the guests. When the long dinner was over, poets and musicians performed.

Here are a few magic tricks you can do to amaze your friends.

Magical Money

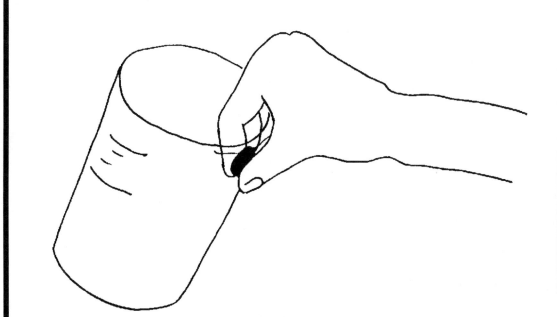

MATERIALS

2 coins
Plastic drinking cup or glass

Tell your friends you are going to show them how to make money appear out of thin air! Sounds pretty impossible, but it's really easy.

Hold the cup with 2 fingers inside the rim. Tuck 2 coins under your fingers so that no one sees them.

Now show your friends that the cup is empty.

Say a few magic words—like abracadabra—wave your hand or a magic wand (see p. 29) over the cup, and let one coin slip from your fingers and fall into the cup.

If your friends dare you to do it again, go ahead. You've got the second coin ready!

MATERIAL

Yarn or string, 2 feet

The trick is to tie a knot in the string by holding the ends of the string and *not letting go*. Try it and you'll see that it's impossible—that is, unless you do the trick this way:

Lay the string out on a table. Cross your arms over and under each other. Pick up the ends of the string in each hand. Now, slowly uncross your arms while holding onto the string. You have tied the magic knot!

Now show your friends, or maybe entertain at the fair.

Magic Knot

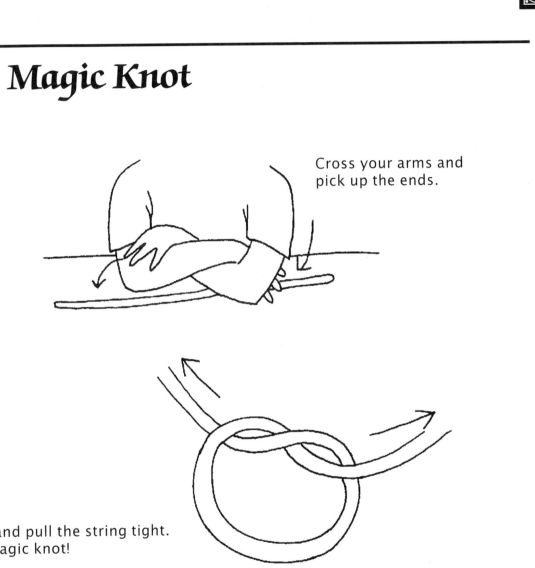

Cross your arms and pick up the ends.

Uncross your arms and pull the string tight. It ties itself into a magic knot!

Coin Catch

MATERIAL

Coin

Bend your elbow and put a coin on your arm. The trick will be to catch the coin with the hand of that same arm!

Practice a bit, and you will be able to do it if you move your hand forward quickly, keeping the fingers cupped to catch the coin as it falls off your arm.

When you get really good at this with one coin, add more coins in a stack to impress your audience.

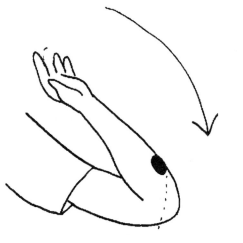

Bring your arm down and catch the coin in your hand.

MATERIALS

3-by-5-inch index card
Scissors

Won't your friends be surprised when you tell them you can put your head through an opening cut in a 3-by-5-inch index card? It's easy, when you know magic. Here's how you do it:

Fold the card in half lengthwise. Snip slits through the fold, but not all way through the other end of the paper. Make about 12 slits.

Turn over the paper and cut new slits from the other side in between the first slits. Cut from the outside toward the fold, but don't cut through the fold.

Snip through the fold on each piece, *except* the first section and last section.

Carefully open and gently pull it apart. The paper will stretch into a large wreath shape that you can easily slip your head through!

Paper Trick

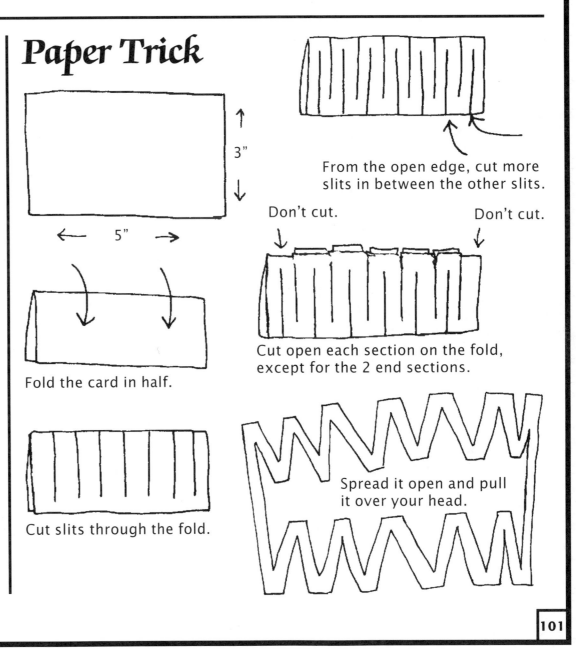

3"

← 5" →

Fold the card in half.

Cut slits through the fold.

From the open edge, cut more slits in between the other slits.

Don't cut.   Don't cut.

Cut open each section on the fold, except for the 2 end sections.

Spread it open and pull it over your head.

Magic Balloon

 This is one trick that would have pleased Merlin, the magician in King Arthur's court, but there weren't any balloons then. Even kings and queens will be surprised when you show them you can poke a straight pin through a balloon, *without popping it!*

Blow a balloon up and tie the end tightly. Tear a small piece of plastic transparent tape and stick it to the side of the balloon. (Don't let your audience see you do that part.)

Now, slowly push the straight pin through the part of the balloon where the piece of tape is attached. The tape seals the hole as you go. The balloon won't pop, but, if you try to put the pin anywhere else on the balloon . . . BANG!

MATERIALS

Balloon
Straight pin
Transparent tape

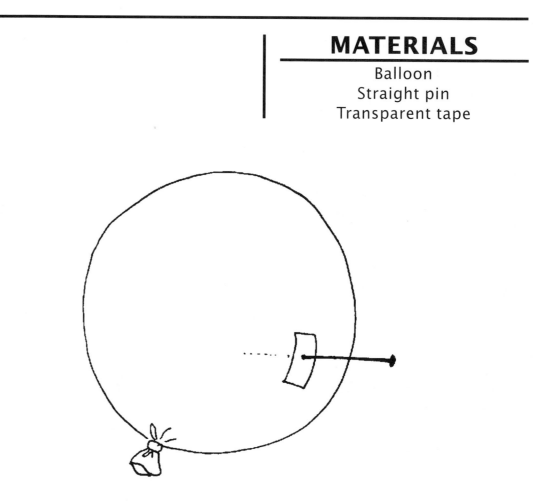

Stick the pin through the tape and into the balloon.

Jumping Jacks

MATERIALS

Card stock or
lightweight cardboard
6 small brass paper fasteners
Pencil
Colored markers
Scissors
Heavy-duty sewing needle
Extra-strong thread
Hole punch or nail

Copy the body parts from the illustration or make up your own design. Add details, color them, and cut them out. Punch holes at the dots. Put the figure together with the brass fasteners. Spread the arms of the fastener on the back side of the puppet so that you won't see them in the front. Fasten them loosely so that the parts move easily.

J umping jacks were sold at the Great Fairs. They were cut from wood and painted by hand. You can make some to use as puppets or to hang up in your room.

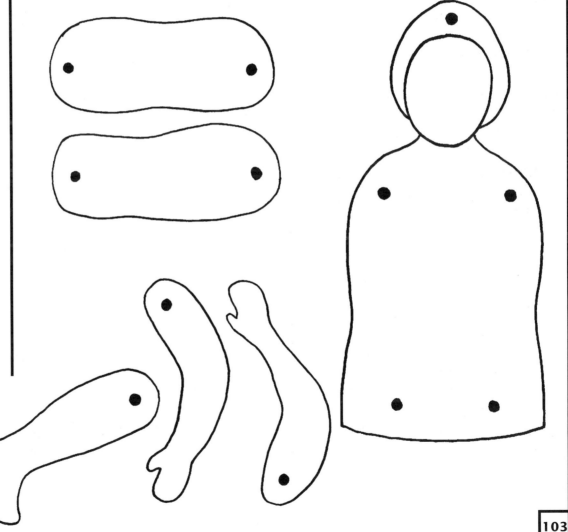

String the jack together on the back. Thread the needle and knot the thread at the end several times. Push the threaded needle through the arm right above the hole. Bring it across the back and into the top of the other arm. Adjust it so the arms are lying straight down, knot the thread tightly and cut off the extra thread.

Do the same thing to the legs. With the legs lying straight down, stitch through the top of the legs above the holes. Knot and cut off the extra thread.

Keep the arms and legs hanging straight, and tie a new piece of thread to the center of the thread between the arms. Tie it in the center of the leg string, too. Let about 8 inches of string hang down.

Punch a hole in the top of the jack's head and tie on a loop of thread that you can hang the jumping jack from.

To make your jumping jack dance, hold its head and gently pull and release the hanging string. As you pull down, the arms and legs move up.

String the jumping jack from the back.

People played tennis without a racquet or net. They batted the ball back and forth with their open hands.

Write It Down!

Monks were Christian missionaries who lived together in walled villages called monasteries. They lived peacefully, growing and making everything they needed for a simple life.

Children of both rich and poor families were sent to live at the monastery and learn to become monks. The first schools were held in monasteries, where children learned to read and write so that they could understand the Bible.

New monasteries needed Bibles, so many monks spent their days copying pages of the Bible (and other books) in order to pass the knowledge on. It took a lot of time and work to copy an entire book, so few people outside the monasteries ever got to see a book.

The children practiced making all the letters in the alphabet. In those days, there were only 23 letters in the alphabet; now we have 26. The teachers asked their students to practice their alphabet by copying sentences that had all the letters in them. Here's one for today's alphabet: "The quick brown fox jumped over the lazy dog's back." Check it out—all 26 letters are in that sentence!

Children in the Middle Ages didn't write English; they learned Latin. They watched the teacher write, and then they traced the letters. The children wrote with pointed sticks on wax slates that could be melted and used over and over. Sometimes a teacher would carve the letters in a block of wood and the children could move their writing sticks in the grooves for practice.

When they weren't in classes with the teachers, the children who lived at the monastery did chores or learned to sing.

Adults who spent their days copying books were called scribes. They worked carefully, copying quickly and neatly in order to pass on the knowledge from books to others.

Scroll & Carrier

You can write whatever you choose on a piece of drawing paper, then roll it up and store it in a special holder. Keep your important letters in it, or make one for a friend and put a special message on the scroll inside.

Trace one end of the tube onto the colored paper. Add 1 inch all around. Cut it out and snip six 1 inch slits around the edge. Fit it to the end of the tube and glue it in place. Wrap and glue colored paper around the rest of the tube to cover it.

Punch 2 holes at the open end and tie on a length of yarn. Now you can hang it from your wall or belt.

Want to pass secret messages on your scroll? See p. 118 for invisible ink.

> Monks who worked as scribes spent all day copying books to make new ones. Their eyesight suffered and they were the first to wear eyeglasses.

MATERIALS

Paper towel tube
Colored construction paper or gift wrap
Yarn
Ruler
Glue
Pencil
Scissors
Hole punch

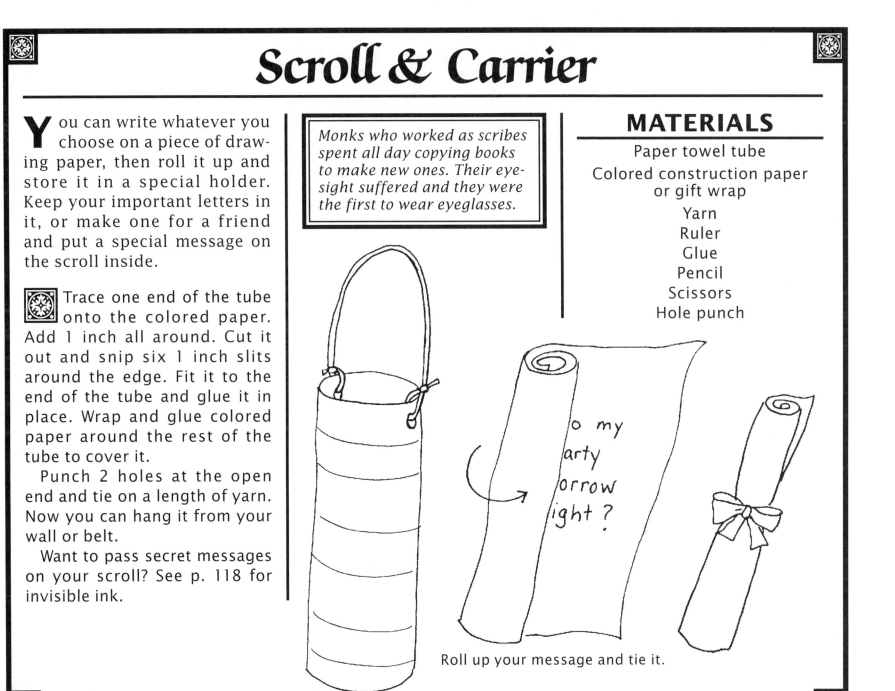

o my
arty
orrow
ight ?

Roll up your message and tie it.

Fancy Writing: Calligraphy

In the Middle Ages, calligraphy was called "fine writing." Most of the books were written by monks. As more people began to want books, scribes were trained to copy the books. Sometimes one person would read aloud while 10 to 20 scribes copied down the words. That meant several copies of a book could be made at one time.

The scribes decorated the pages of the books beautifully. They were usually copying the Bible, so they wanted to make the pages as glorious as possible.

One scribe would pencil in the design, another would draw it in, and another colored it with inks.

They had to learn how to make the letters perfectly and how to make their own inks and pens.

You can copy the letters shown here, or make up some fancy letters of your own.

MATERIALS

Calligraphy pen or felt-tipped marker
Paper

Place a sheet of thin paper over the letters in the illustration and trace them with your pen. Hold the pen straight, and don't turn it as you write. Begin at the top of each letter and pull the line down to the bottom of the letter.

The scribes held their pens straight up.

This style is Early Gothic from the 11th and 12th centuries.

You can add *serifs* to your letters. Serifs are the lines added at the top and bottom of letters. Draw them on after you've written the letter.

To keep your paper clean, keep a piece of scrap paper under your hand as you write.

The decorated pages of books were called *illuminated.* They had a beautiful shine, because paint made from gold was used on them. You can use gold or silver felt marking pens to add this shiny touch to your pages.

Scribes decorated book pages by coloring one large letter first on each page. They drew little colored pictures of angels, flowers, vines, butterflies, bees, ladybugs, dragonflies, caterpillars, and snails around the border and between the words.

Draw serifs in steps.

1 2 3

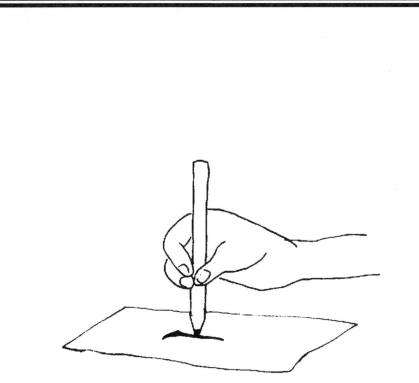

It helps to hold the pen up straight.

Decorate Some Notepaper

MATERIALS

Blue-lined graph paper
Black pen
White correction fluid
Colored pencils

Draw on the graph paper with a black pen. If you make a mistake, cover it with a drop of white office correction fluid. When you are finished, take it to a copy center and have several copies made. Then color in the design area with colored pencils or fine-tipped markers.

Use this beautiful notepaper to write to your friends and relatives.

Decorate letters like the Irish scribes once did.

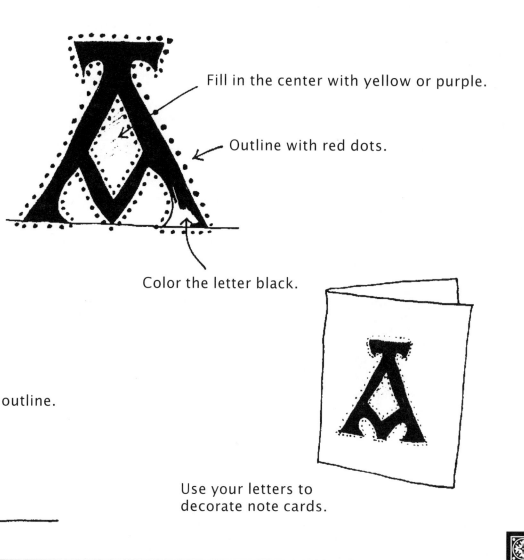

Fill in the center with yellow or purple.

Outline with red dots.

Color the letter black.

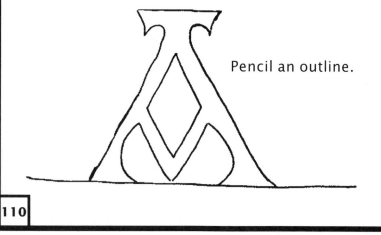

Pencil an outline.

Use your letters to decorate note cards.

Here are some designs used for borders in the Middle Ages.

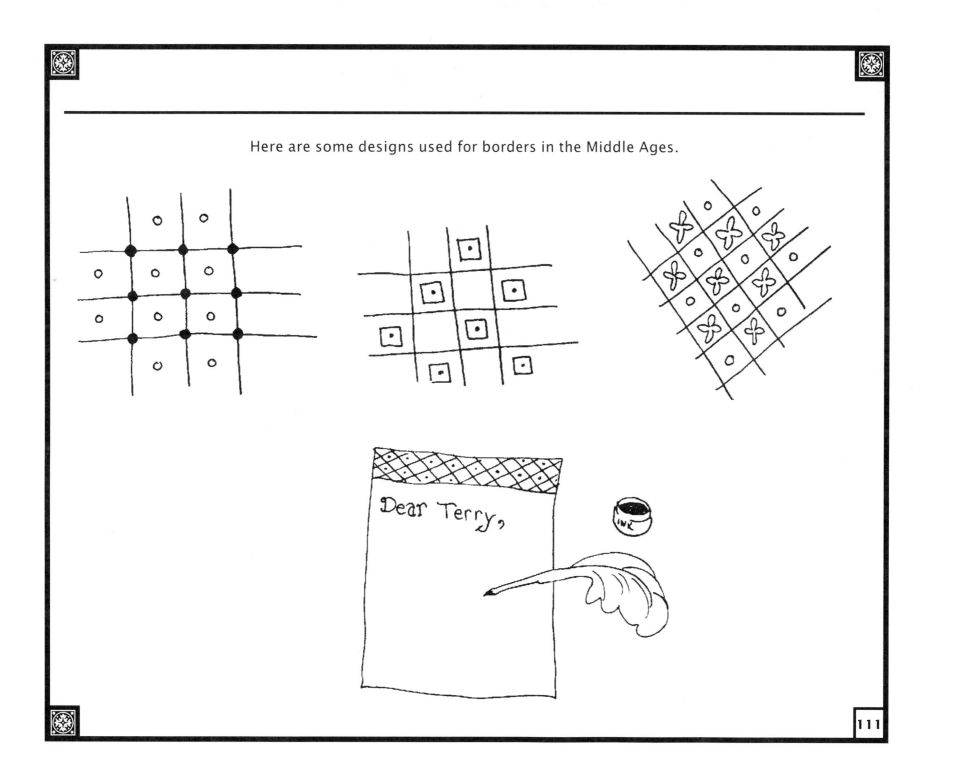

Printing

Everything changed when movable type was invented. Monks didn't have to spend their lives copying books. Printers could arrange letters to print book pages quickly and easily. They made more books, cheaper. Everyone could have books!

Movable type was created by cutting letters or words into wooden blocks that could be used to print with ink again and again. Johannes Gutenberg, of Germany, first used wooden blocks but later invented movable metal type that he cast in molds.

Eventually, the idea of using movable type caught on throughout Europe, and suddenly the world was changed. This technique made knowledge available to many, instead of just a privileged few. It was the greatest cultural event in the history of the world because ideas and enlightenment could free people from ignorance.

Printed Design

Glue string or wire to cardboard scraps.

Dip in paint and print.

MATERIALS

Cardboard,
about 4 by 4 inches
String or paper clips
Tempera paint
Paper
Glue
Shallow tray

Dip the string in the glue and arrange it on the cardboard in a shape you like, or bend the paper clips into a design and glue them down.

After the glue has dried, squirt some paint on the tray. Dip the string or wire design into the paint, and then press it onto the paper to print a design.

MATERIALS

Cardboard
Alphabet pasta
Paper
Glue
Ink pad or markers

 Cut the cardboard into 1-by-2-inch pieces. Glue the pasta letters down to make words. Remember to glue on the letters backwards so that they print correctly. When the glue dries, press your stamp in ink or rub the letters with a marking pen. Press it onto paper, and you're printing!

Ink was made from soot mixed with tree sap and acid. Pens were made from goose feathers or reeds. Vellum (calf's skin) or parchment (sheep's skin) was used instead of paper.

Printed Words

Glue alphabet pasta to cardboard scraps. Color with a dark marker and press on paper.

Paper

When people were copying books by hand they wrote on pages made from parchment. Printing didn't work very well on parchment, and it was very expensive. About the time the printing press was created, paper was discovered by Europeans.

The first people to make paper were the Chinese. They kept the idea secret until the sixth century. Then Arabs captured paper-makers and forced them to tell how it was done. It was 1,000 years before the idea spread to Europe.

The Chinese had used rags to make paper. It didn't take long before papermakers in Europe ran out of rags and needed something else to make paper with. A person noticed how wasps chewed up tiny mouthfuls of wood to make their papery nests. It wasn't long before people began cutting down trees, grinding them up to a pulp, and making paper from them.

That's still the way paper is made today.

You can use an electric blender to churn up a pulp of torn newspapers and water. Pour it over a piece of screen (buy at a hardware store) held over a plastic dishpan. The pulp will remain on the screen and can be pressed and dried between two pieces of muslin fabric, with a dry steam iron.

The books in monastery libraries were so valuable that they were chained to the shelves. Many of the monasteries and books were burned by invading armies.

Marbled Paper

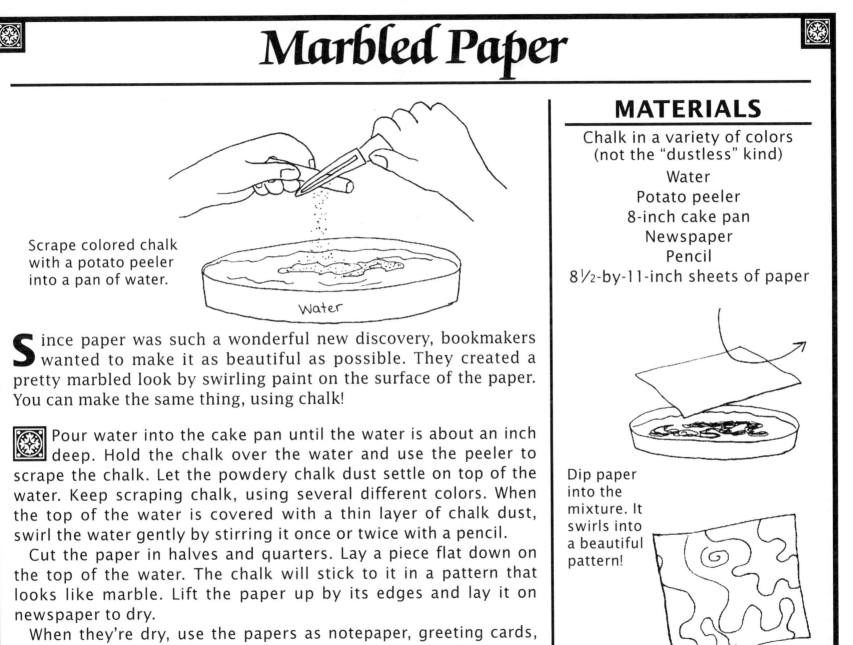

Scrape colored chalk with a potato peeler into a pan of water.

Water

MATERIALS

Chalk in a variety of colors (not the "dustless" kind)
Water
Potato peeler
8-inch cake pan
Newspaper
Pencil
8½-by-11-inch sheets of paper

Dip paper into the mixture. It swirls into a beautiful pattern!

Since paper was such a wonderful new discovery, bookmakers wanted to make it as beautiful as possible. They created a pretty marbled look by swirling paint on the surface of the paper. You can make the same thing, using chalk!

Pour water into the cake pan until the water is about an inch deep. Hold the chalk over the water and use the peeler to scrape the chalk. Let the powdery chalk dust settle on top of the water. Keep scraping chalk, using several different colors. When the top of the water is covered with a thin layer of chalk dust, swirl the water gently by stirring it once or twice with a pencil.

Cut the paper in halves and quarters. Lay a piece flat down on the top of the water. The chalk will stick to it in a pattern that looks like marble. Lift the paper up by its edges and lay it on newspaper to dry.

When they're dry, use the papers as notepaper, greeting cards, gift wrap for tiny packages, origami papers, or bookmarks.

You can also decorate white paper lunch sacks to use as gift bags.

Make a Book

MATERIALS

8½-by-11-inch white paper

Sheet 8½-by-11-inch
colored gift wrap,
construction paper,
or wallpaper

Two 6-by-9-inch
cardboard pieces

12-by-16-inch woven fabric

Scissors

Glue

Darning needle and heavy
thread, or long-armed stapler

 Lay 10 pieces of paper in a stack. Place the gift wrap or other fancy paper at the bottom of the stack, with the pretty side facing the white papers. This piece is called the *endpaper.* Sew or staple through the center of all the pages. (You can also use a sewing machine. If you do, set the stitch length to make the longest stitch possible and sew slowly.)

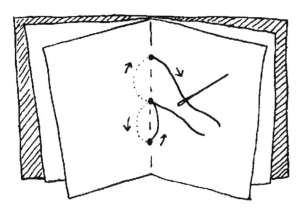

Stitch blank
paper together
on top of the
endpaper.

In medieval days people spent time reading books written by their ancestors. They treasured these family diaries and journals. You might be able to find some of these old books in the local library or historical society. You can start your own family history journal in a handmade book.

Just think, your own children's children may someday treasure the words you write about your life today!

People spent a lot of time writing their memoirs and reading diaries handed down in the family. They were kept in locked chests in the family bedroom.

Book covers were made as beautiful as possible. Some were carved in leather, embroidered in velvet, and decorated with gold, pearls, and jewels.

6" x 9" cardboard

6" x 9" cardboard

12" x 16" fabric

Glue

Fold and glue fabric to the cardboard pieces.

If you are stitching by hand, poke the needle through the papers and stitch as shown in the drawing. Don't pull the thread too tightly. Knot the thread when you are finished, and trim the end. Set the pages aside.

Lay the fabric with the wrong side facing up. Center the cardboard pieces on it leaving half an inch space between them.

Trim the corners of the fabric away. This will help the corners lie flat when they are glued.

Spread glue on the edges of the cardboard and fold the fabric over it. Press down neatly.

Spread glue over the rest of the cover where the cardboard is showing, except on the fabric lying between the two cardboard pieces. This part in the middle will become your book's "spine."

Lay the pages onto the cover, pressing the back of the endpapers into the glue. Open and close the book to adjust the cover smoothly. Wipe away any extra glue so that the pages won't stick to the cover.

After it dries, it's ready for you to fill with drawings and stories.

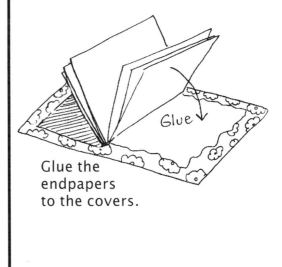

Glue

Glue the endpapers to the covers.

Secret Letters in Invisible Ink

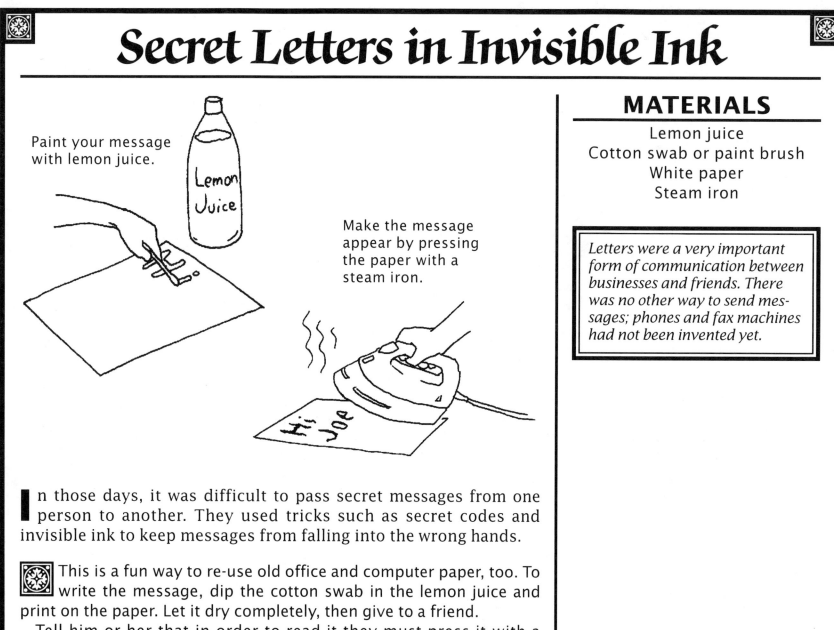

Paint your message with lemon juice.

Lemon Juice

Make the message appear by pressing the paper with a steam iron.

Hi Joe

MATERIALS

Lemon juice
Cotton swab or paint brush
White paper
Steam iron

Letters were a very important form of communication between businesses and friends. There was no other way to send messages; phones and fax machines had not been invented yet.

In those days, it was difficult to pass secret messages from one person to another. They used tricks such as secret codes and invisible ink to keep messages from falling into the wrong hands.

This is a fun way to re-use old office and computer paper, too. To write the message, dip the cotton swab in the lemon juice and print on the paper. Let it dry completely, then give to a friend.

Tell him or her that in order to read it they must press it with a warm steam iron. The heat will bring out the "secret" writing, and the words will turn brown.

Fold an Envelope

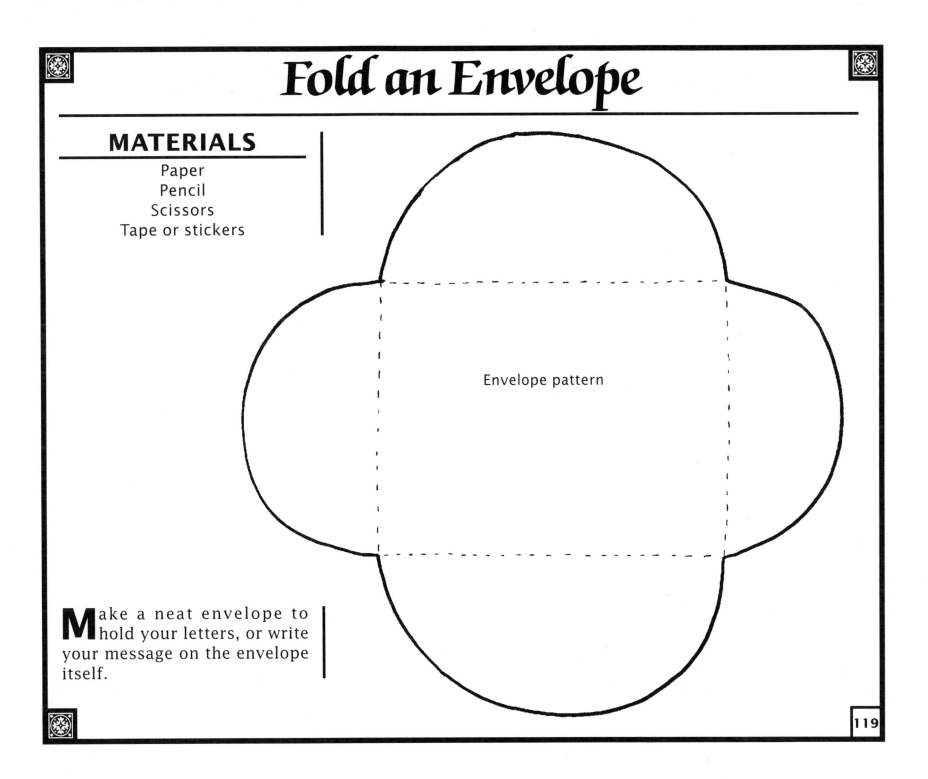

MATERIALS
Paper
Pencil
Scissors
Tape or stickers

Envelope pattern

Make a neat envelope to hold your letters, or write your message on the envelope itself.

Your homemade envelopes can be any size and can be made of any kind of paper—comics, gift wrap, wallpaper, and even shopping bags.

Find something that's shaped like a square or rectangle—a book, notepad, or small box. Trace the shape onto the center of your paper, and then draw large half circles along the sides. Cut it out and fold the curved sides to the center along the rectangle outline. Overlap the edges and seal with a sticker or a small piece of tape. People in the Middle Ages used a drop of wax to seal their envelopes.

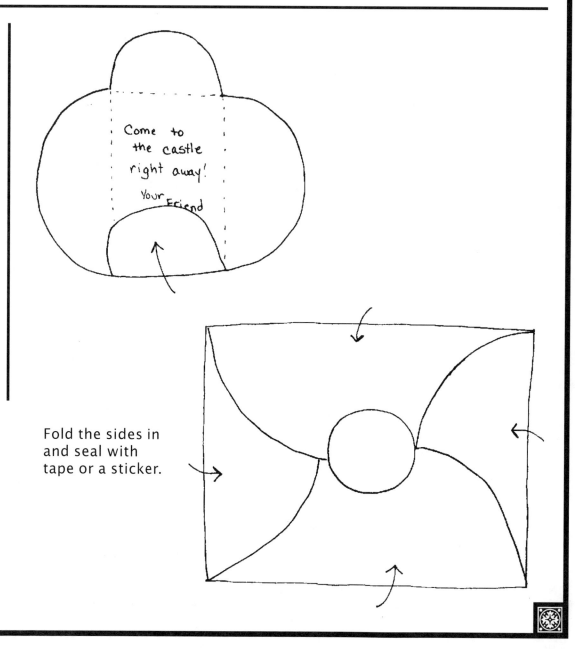

Fold the sides in and seal with tape or a sticker.

Maps

Marco Polo made a great journey across Asia to see the Chinese emperor during the Middle Ages. He learned about many new ways of doing things. After he returned home to Europe, his stories and maps made other people interested in traveling. They wanted to travel great distances by ship, to discover new lands, and to trade for exotic things from far away.

In order to travel, people wanted maps made by those who had been there before. Sometimes no one knew what was in an area of a map, because no one had gone there before. They filled those areas of a map with fanciful drawings of what they guessed might be there.

 Draw a map for yourself that shows where you've traveled. What is the farthest distance you've been? Show this place on your map, and then draw what you think lies beyond that place. What do you think it looks like out there, in the unknown world?

Compass

When travelers went long distances by ship they had to travel at night, when they couldn't tell the direction they were going. They also were beyond the sight of land for many days. They needed some way to tell if they were traveling in the right direction, so they invented a compass. We still use compasses to tell us where the four directions lie: north, south, east, and west. Since they are always in the same place, we can tell where we are headed if we know where at least one of the four directions lies.

Poke the nail through the center of the cork, lengthwise. You may want to break the cork in half if your nail is short. Make sure that some of the nail sticks out both ends.

Line up the electrons inside the nail by pulling it across the magnet several times. Pull in the same direction with each stroke.

Drop it into the pan of water and watch what happens. It will float and bob around a bit, and finally it will stop. The nail will point in the direction of north. It's lined itself up with the North Pole (a magnetic point on the earth).

Try it again—every time, it will end up pointing north.

This was a useful way for travelers to chart their travels into the unknown world as they drew maps that those who came after them could follow.

MATERIALS

Nail
Cork or Styrofoam
Small magnet
Plastic or glass pan of water

Put in a non-metal pan of water and it will point north.

Magnet

Push a nail through a cork.
Stroke it against the magnet several times.

A Little Geometry

By the end of the medieval period, European people began to study math, which they learned from the works of ancient Greeks and neighboring Arabs.

Make some paper models like the ones mathematicians studied in the Middle Ages.

MATERIALS

Paper
Pencil
Scissors
Glue

A *tetrahedron* is a shape with 4 faces. It's easy to make one. Draw and cut out 4 triangles from the pattern in the drawing. Fold the tabs back. Spread glue on the tabs and press them together to make a pyramid shape: 3 triangles for the pyramid and 1 for the base. You can glue the tabs inside the model or press them together outside.

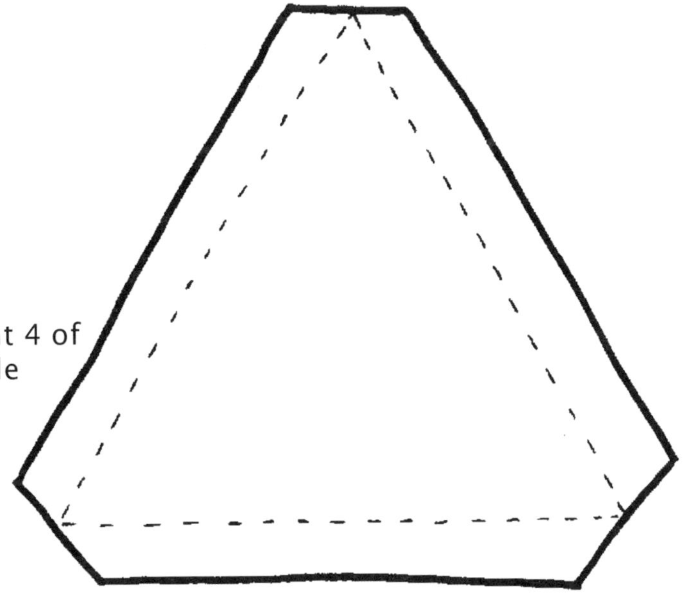

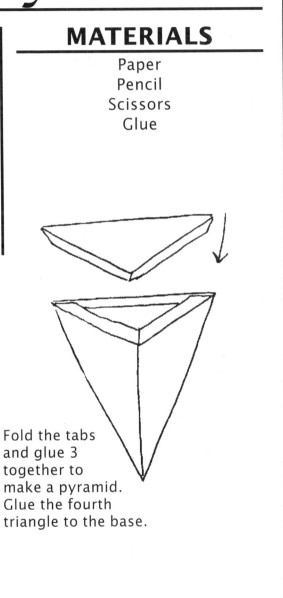

Trace and cut 4 of these triangle shapes.

Fold the tabs and glue 3 together to make a pyramid. Glue the fourth triangle to the base.

Now make an *octahedron*—a shape with 8 faces. Use 8 triangles. Glue 4 together for the top, and 4 more for the bottom. Then glue them together around the middle.

You can use different sizes and shapes of triangles, as long as they are identical to one another.

Hang your models from the ceiling with a piece of thread and a thumbtack, or hang them from a Christmas tree with paper clips. You can tuck tiny gifts or candy surprises inside, and give them as party favors or presents.

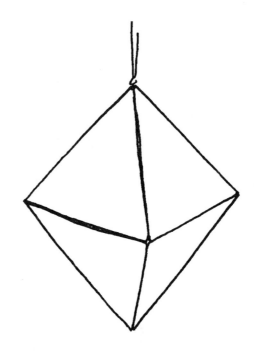

Use 8 to make an octahedron.

Arts & Crafts

In the Middle Ages, everything was handmade; there were no factories. If people couldn't make the item themselves, they had to trade for it or do without. People who excelled at making a craft could make items for trade or work for royalty in a castle.

During the Middle Ages, *guilds* were created. A guild was a group of artists or craftspeople who all made the same things. Guilds protected and encouraged the work of their members. After working for a master craftsmaker for several years, an apprentice would create the best item he or she could. The item was presented to the members of the guild, who inspected it to see if it was done well. If so, the apprentice became a *master,* and the item was his or her *masterpiece.*

Gather together a few materials and have fun creating some masterpieces of your own!

Twist Some Wire Jewelry

Fine jewelry worn in the Middle Ages was made from metals such as gold and silver. Artists heated it and pounded or twisted it into shapes, or they melted the metal and poured it into molds.

Make yourself some interesting jewelry by wrapping and twisting metal wire into necklaces, armbands, rings, or anything you like.

MATERIALS

Thin wire
(copper or brass looks best)
Old scissors
Long-nosed pliers or tweezers

Try making a necklace first. Bend a piece to fit around your neck and bend the ends so they can be hooked together.

Cut short pieces of wire and twist them to make pendants to hang from the necklace.

Bend small pieces into loops and connect them to make chains. Link them together and create necklaces, bracelets, and ankle bracelets.

Make a ring by bending a wire around your finger and twisting the ends into spirals.

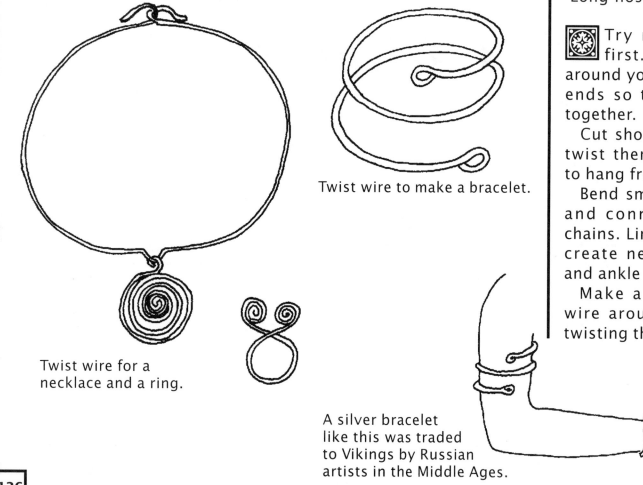

Twist wire to make a bracelet.

Twist wire for a necklace and a ring.

A silver bracelet like this was traded to Vikings by Russian artists in the Middle Ages.

Embroider a Bookmark

MATERIALS

Fabric:
muslin, broadcloth, or felt
Embroidery needle and thread
Scissors
Pencil
Glue

Embroidery was an important skill taught to every girl. Clothing, bedding, book covers, and wall hangings were covered with beautiful, hand-stitched designs.

Cut two pieces of fabric, about 6 by 2 inches.

Pencil a design lightly on one piece of the fabric. Use the simple design shown here from Ireland, or make up one.

Thread the needle with a length of thread and knot the ends.

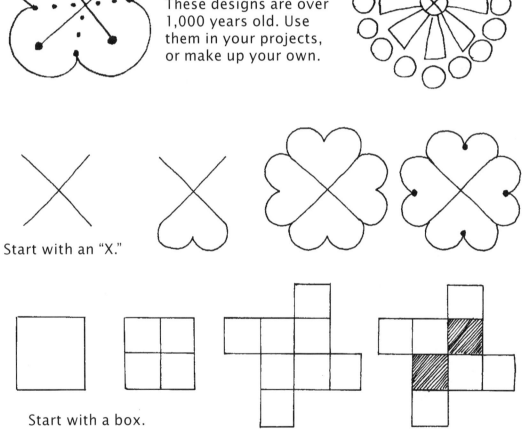

These designs are over 1,000 years old. Use them in your projects, or make up your own.

Start with an "X."

Start with a box.

127

Stitch over the design using the "chain stitch" illustrated here. When you're finished, tie the ends in a knot on the back side.

Glue the other fabric piece onto the back as a lining.

When it's dry, embroider around the edges with the "blanket stitch."

You can use embroidery stitches to decorate handkerchiefs, socks, shirt collars, or jeans.

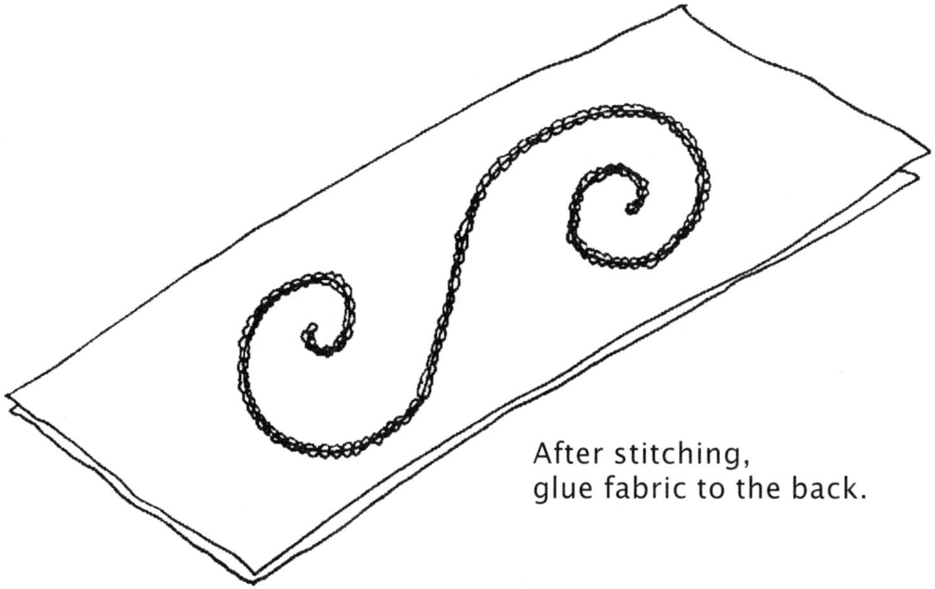

After stitching,
glue fabric to the back.

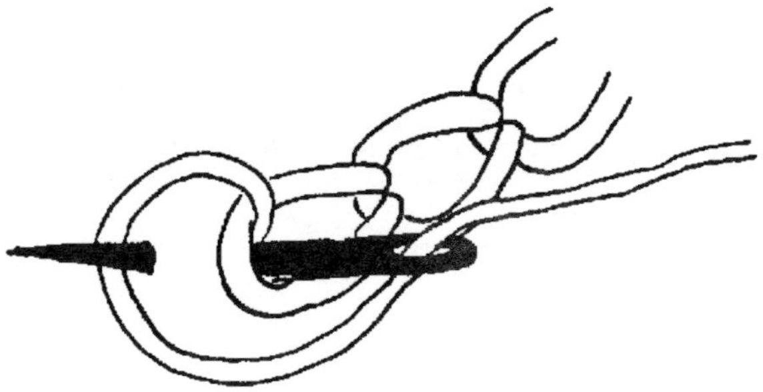

Chain stitch

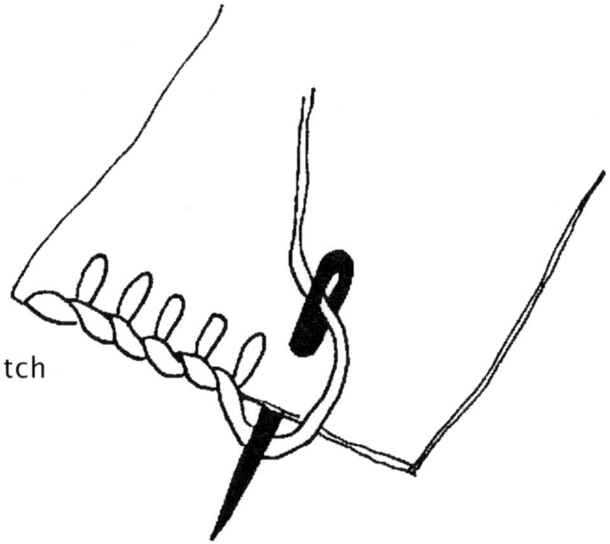

Blanket stitch

For Larger Embroidery Projects

Your bookmark is small, so no embroidery hoop is needed; but, for larger projects, you'll need a hoop to stretch the fabric smooth as you stitch. You can make one out of a plastic margarine tub.

Cut away the center from the lid of the container. Then, cut the rim off the tub, cutting close to the rim.

Slip the fabric between the two pieces and snap them together. You can also use this hoop as a mini-frame by hanging your needlework in it for display.

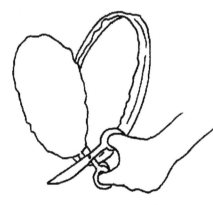

Cut the center out of the lid of a margarine tub.

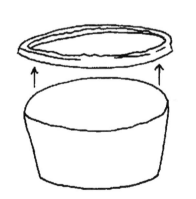

Cut the rim off the top of the tub.

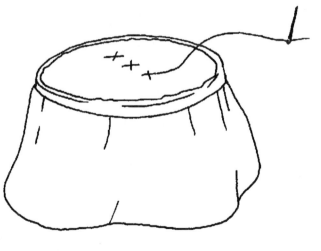

Snap the pieces together over your embroidery project.

Lady's Pincushion

Ladies in the medieval days cherished their precious needles and pins. They would have enjoyed this cushion to keep them in. You can easily make several pincushions for yourself and for any friends or relatives who like to sew.

Cut a 2-inch strip and a 12-inch circle from the fabric.

Glue the strip to the outside of the tuna can, folding the edge into the can.

Wad two handfuls of stuffing and put them in the center of the fabric circle. Pull the circle up around the stuffing and fasten it tightly with the rubber band. Squish it into shape to fit the can.

Squirt glue along the sides and bottom of the inside of the can. Press the cushion into place and let it dry.

Glue pieces of ribbons, lace, or other trim to the can. Add a ribbon bow or a tiny fake flower.

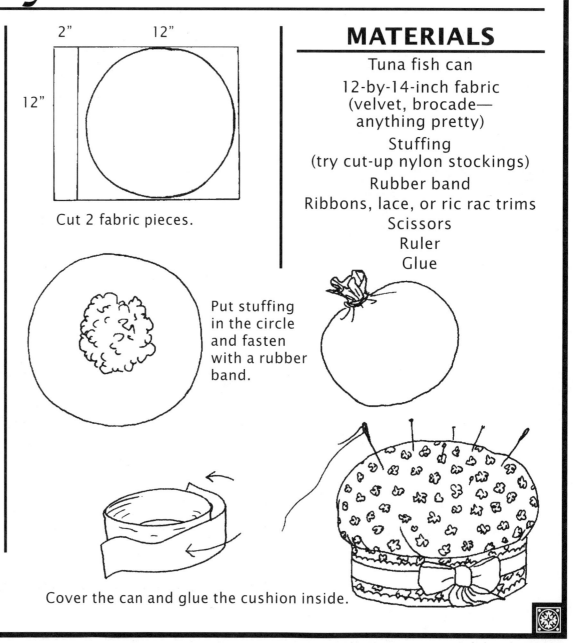

2"   12"

12"

Cut 2 fabric pieces.

Put stuffing in the circle and fasten with a rubber band.

Cover the can and glue the cushion inside.

MATERIALS

Tuna fish can
12-by-14-inch fabric
(velvet, brocade—anything pretty)
Stuffing
(try cut-up nylon stockings)
Rubber band
Ribbons, lace, or ric rac trims
Scissors
Ruler
Glue

"Stained Glass" Paintings

MATERIALS

Construction paper
or tagboard
White glue (in a squirt bottle)
Black tempera paint
Watercolor paints and brush

 Try to find an old bottle of glue that's almost empty. Take the lid off the glue bottle and add enough black tempera paint to tint the glue black. Shake it a few times so the glue and paint are completely mixed.

Squirt several lines of glue over the paper. You can draw a design with a pencil first and then squirt the black glue over the lines, or you can just squirt out your design free-form.

After the glue dries, paint in the spaces with different colors of watercolor paint.

Craftsmen made stained glass in small pieces, and used them to make beautiful windows in churches and castles. They made the glass in different colors and then cut it into small pieces to fit a design. Bands of lead held the glass pieces in place.

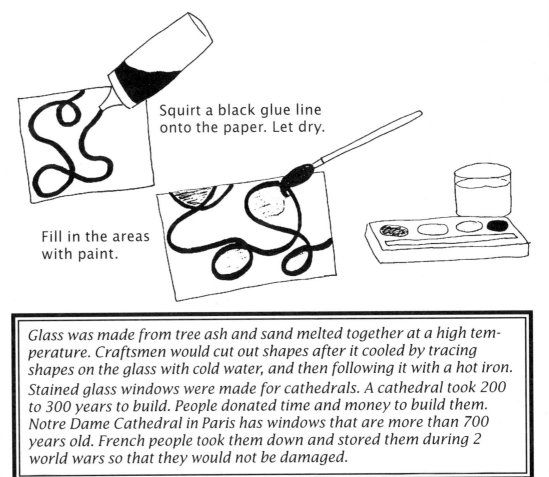

Squirt a black glue line onto the paper. Let dry.

Fill in the areas with paint.

Glass was made from tree ash and sand melted together at a high temperature. Craftsmen would cut out shapes after it cooled by tracing shapes on the glass with cold water, and then following it with a hot iron.

Stained glass windows were made for cathedrals. A cathedral took 200 to 300 years to build. People donated time and money to build them. Notre Dame Cathedral in Paris has windows that are more than 700 years old. French people took them down and stored them during 2 world wars so that they would not be damaged.

Try a Triptych

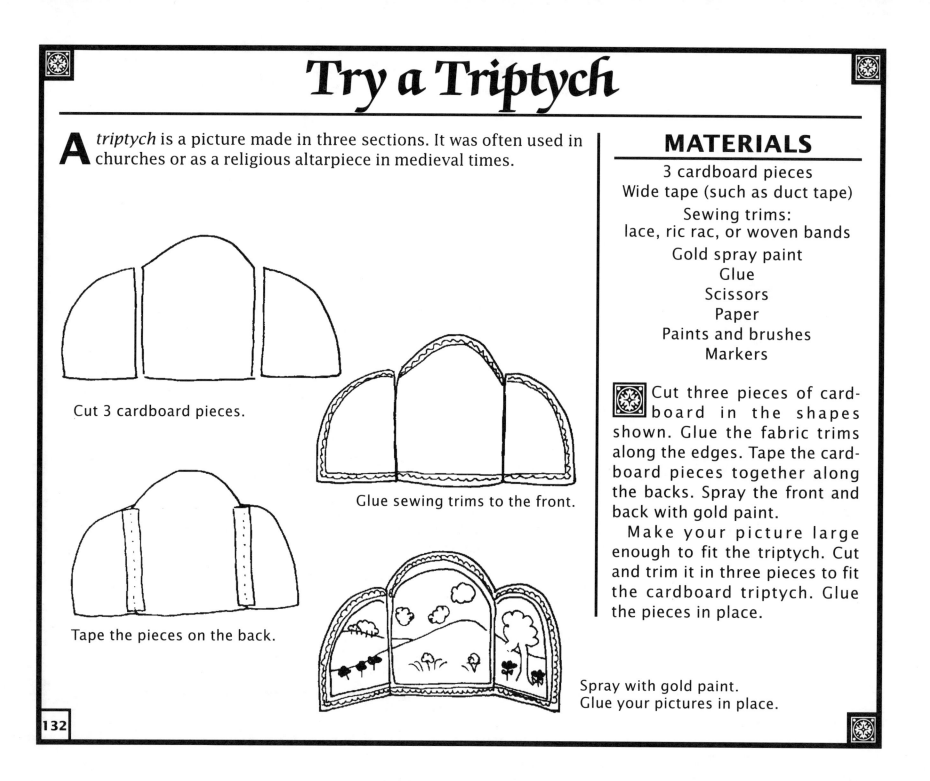

A *triptych* is a picture made in three sections. It was often used in churches or as a religious altarpiece in medieval times.

Cut 3 cardboard pieces.

Glue sewing trims to the front.

Tape the pieces on the back.

Spray with gold paint.
Glue your pictures in place.

MATERIALS

3 cardboard pieces
Wide tape (such as duct tape)
Sewing trims:
lace, ric rac, or woven bands
Gold spray paint
Glue
Scissors
Paper
Paints and brushes
Markers

Cut three pieces of cardboard in the shapes shown. Glue the fabric trims along the edges. Tape the cardboard pieces together along the backs. Spray the front and back with gold paint.

Make your picture large enough to fit the triptych. Cut and trim it in three pieces to fit the cardboard triptych. Glue the pieces in place.

Knit a Scarf

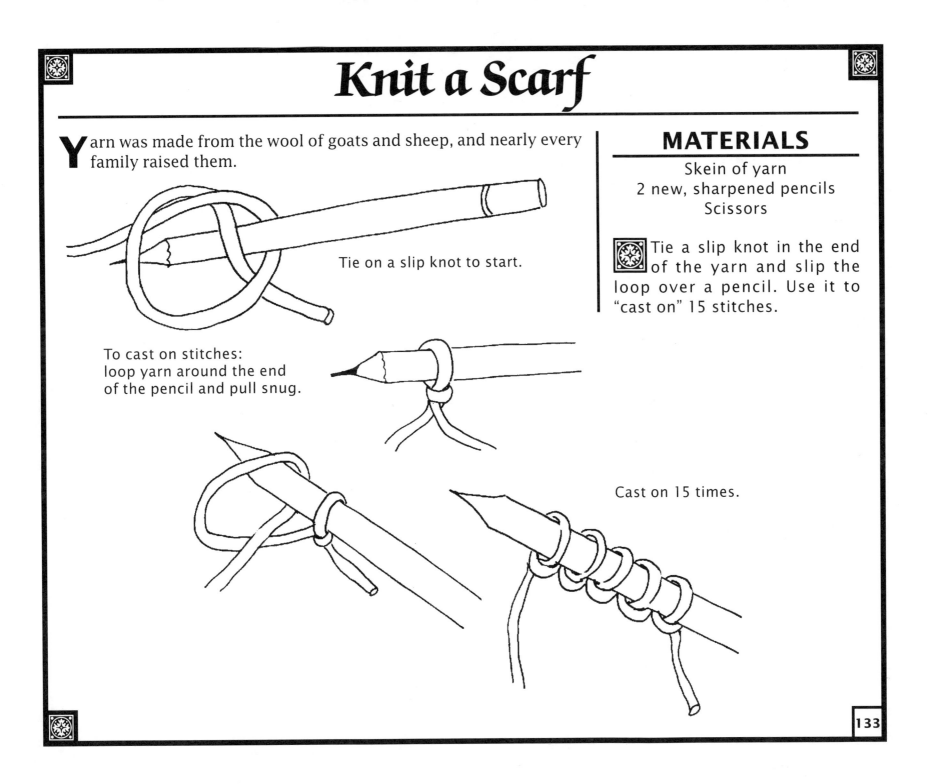

Yarn was made from the wool of goats and sheep, and nearly every family raised them.

Tie on a slip knot to start.

To cast on stitches:
loop yarn around the end
of the pencil and pull snug.

Cast on 15 times.

MATERIALS

Skein of yarn
2 new, sharpened pencils
Scissors

Tie a slip knot in the end of the yarn and slip the loop over a pencil. Use it to "cast on" 15 stitches.

Begin knitting by poking the pencil into the stitch, wrapping yarn around it, and pulling it through the stitch to make a new loop. Say to yourself as you work: "poke—wrap around—pull through—slide off."

Keep knitting row after row until the scarf is as long as you want. "Bind off" at the end, and knot the last stitch.

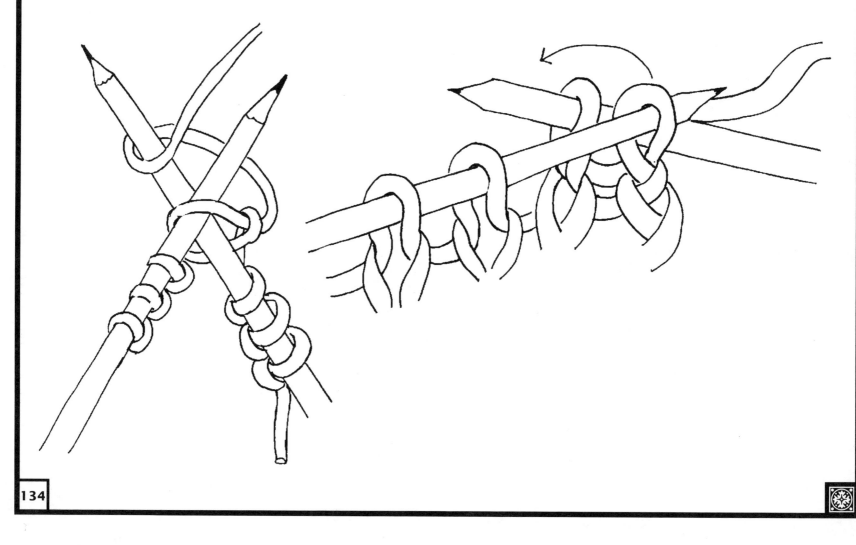

Repeat for every stitch in the row, knotting the yarn in the last stitch so your piece won't unravel.

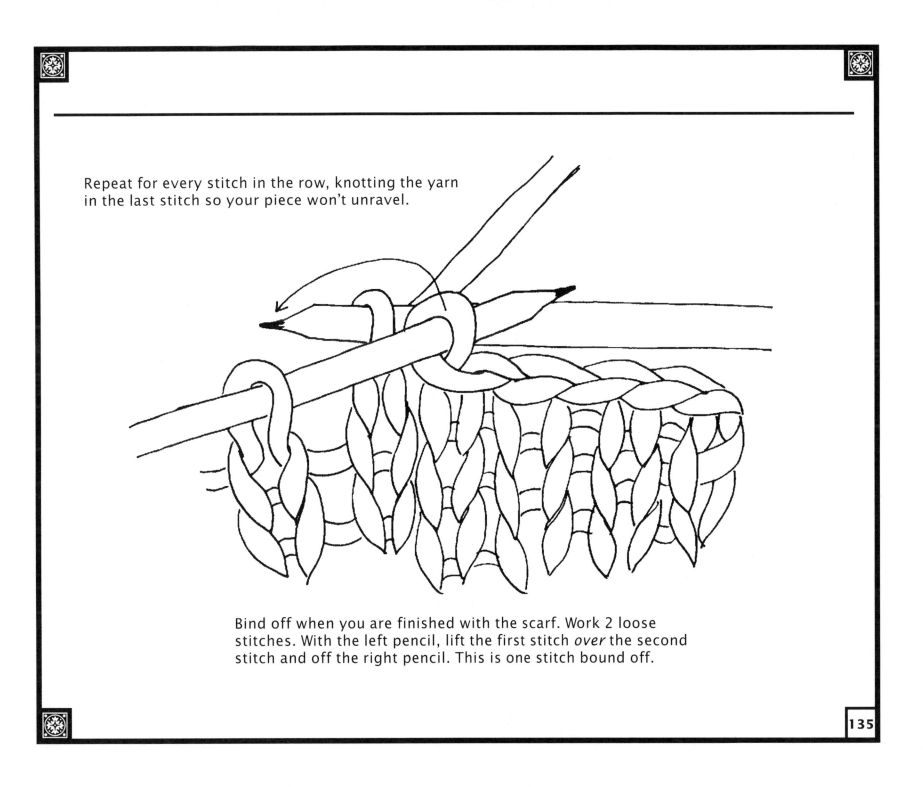

Bind off when you are finished with the scarf. Work 2 loose stitches. With the left pencil, lift the first stitch *over* the second stitch and off the right pencil. This is one stitch bound off.

You can wrap and tie some yarn tassels to put on the corners if you want. Wrap yarn around one hand, hold it with your thumb while you cut the loops. Gather the tops together and tie with a string. Wrap and tie another short string around the tassel.

Tie with a short piece of yarn.

MAKE A TASSEL

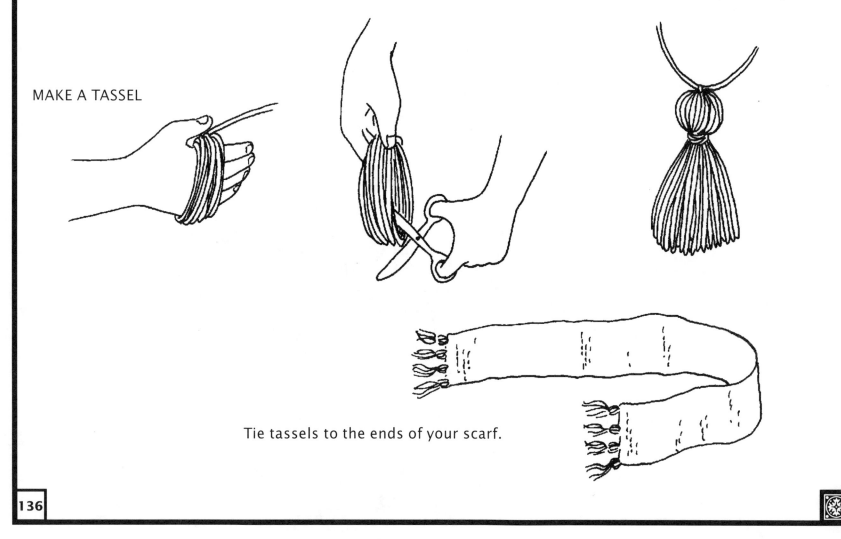

Tie tassels to the ends of your scarf.

Crochet a Bag

MATERIALS

Yarn
Crochet hook, size H or larger
Yarn needle*

*You can make a yarn needle
by cutting a needle shape from
a plastic bottle and poking
a hole in the end

Make a slip knot near the end of the yarn.

Slip the hook into the loop and begin pulling stitches through.

Hold the hook as if it was a pencil. Wrap yarn over the end of the hook, catch it with the hook, and pull through the loop that's left on the hook.

Make a chain of 38 loops by catching the strand of yarn with the hook and pulling it through the loop.

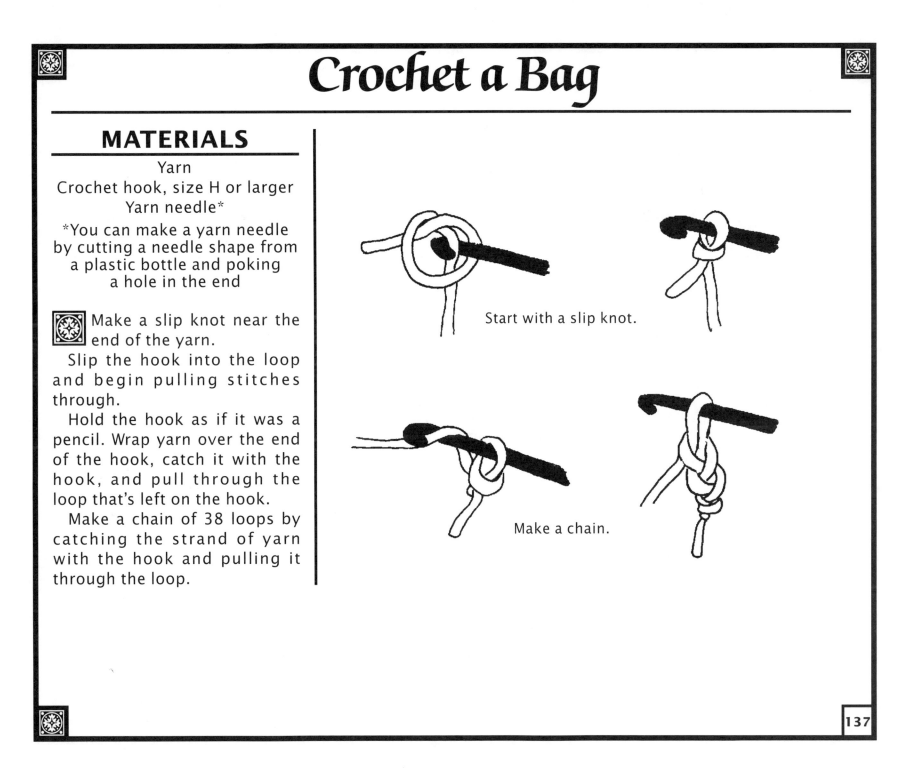

Start with a slip knot.

Make a chain.

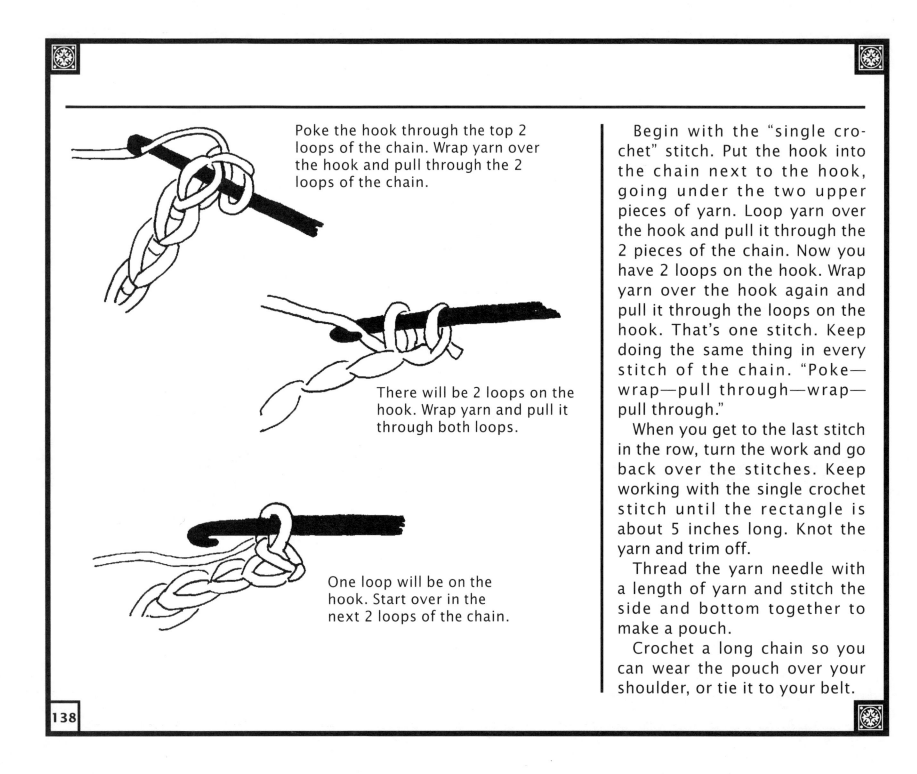

Poke the hook through the top 2 loops of the chain. Wrap yarn over the hook and pull through the 2 loops of the chain.

There will be 2 loops on the hook. Wrap yarn and pull it through both loops.

One loop will be on the hook. Start over in the next 2 loops of the chain.

Begin with the "single crochet" stitch. Put the hook into the chain next to the hook, going under the two upper pieces of yarn. Loop yarn over the hook and pull it through the 2 pieces of the chain. Now you have 2 loops on the hook. Wrap yarn over the hook again and pull it through the loops on the hook. That's one stitch. Keep doing the same thing in every stitch of the chain. "Poke—wrap—pull through—wrap—pull through."

When you get to the last stitch in the row, turn the work and go back over the stitches. Keep working with the single crochet stitch until the rectangle is about 5 inches long. Knot the yarn and trim off.

Thread the yarn needle with a length of yarn and stitch the side and bottom together to make a pouch.

Crochet a long chain so you can wear the pouch over your shoulder, or tie it to your belt.

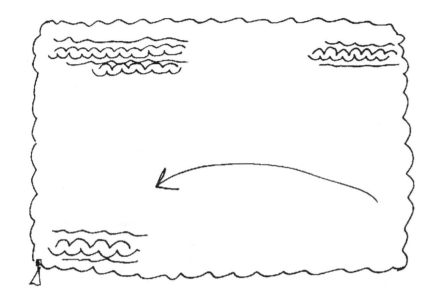

Fold in half and stitch bottom and side.

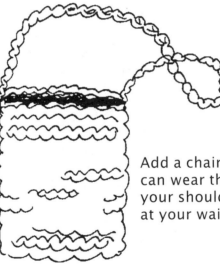

Add a chain so you can wear the bag over your shoulder or tie it at your waist.

Over & Under Weaving

Paper Placemat

Medieval people wove with wool, but you can use paper to make a placemat.

You can use colorful magazine pages or 2 colors of construction paper.

Cut the first sheet in 1-inch strips.

Fold the other sheet in half lengthwise. Cut slits 1 inch apart, cutting through the fold but stopping half an inch from the other end of the paper.

Unfold the paper, and you can begin weaving the strips through the slits.

To weave, put the strip over, then under, the slits. Do the next strip under first, then over. This makes a pattern, going over and under every other piece.

Glue or staple the ends in place when you are finished. To make your placemat last a long time you can cover it with clear adhesive plastic (such as Contac) or have it laminated.

MATERIALS

2 sheets of paper
Scissors
Glue or stapler
Clear adhesive plastic
(optional)

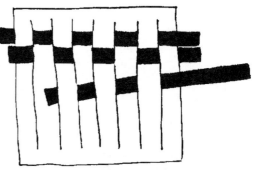

Weave the strips over and under in sections.

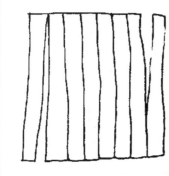

Cut 1 sheet in 1-inch strips.

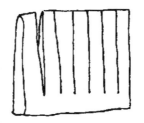

Fold the other sheet and cut in 1-inch sections. Stop cutting 1/2 inch from the edge.

MATERIALS

Cardboard square or rectangle
Yarn in various colors
Pencil
Ruler
Nail
Scissors
Tape

People in guilds took care of each other, had special songs and ceremonies, and tried to keep their craft a mystery, so that few would know how to do it.

Tapestry

A tapestry is a woven picture. People hung them on castle walls to make the cold stone rooms pretty and warm. Make a small yarn tapestry to hang on your own wall.

Use the ruler and pencil to mark dots every ½ inch along 2 facing ends of the cardboard.

Poke holes through the dots with the nail. Now you have a loom.

Wrap a piece of tape tightly on the end of the yarn to stiffen it so that it will go through the holes easily. Thread it through the holes, up and down across the front of the loom. Tie the ends in back.

Now you have "warped" the loom, and you're ready to weave.

Begin at the bottom of the loom and weave the yarn over and under the warp yarns. When you want to change colors of yarn, knot and hide the ends behind the weaving.

When you have finished, you can leave the weaving on the cardboard, or you can clip the warp yarns two at a time, and knot them together.

String the loom.

Make a yarn needle by cutting a shape from an empty plastic bottle. Thread and use to weave in and out on the loom.

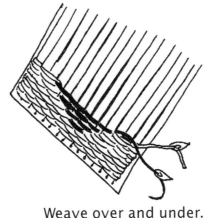

Weave over and under.

141

Sculpt a Statue

Artists created statues to decorate churches. They used wood, metal, ivory, or stone to make tiny figures, or very large ones. You can try your hand at making a small statue.

MATERIALS

Plaster of paris
Mixing container
(plastic bucket or coffee can)
Stirring stick or spoon
Water
Quart milk carton
Sculpting tools:
serrated plastic knife, spoon, toothpick, paper clip, old toothbrush, or nail
Sponge or paper towel

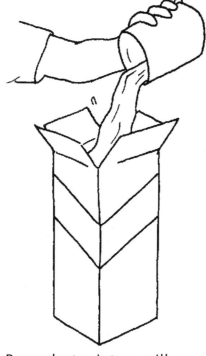

Pour plaster into a milk carton. Let it harden.

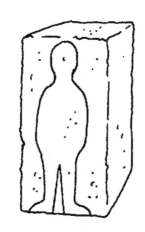

Remove the carton and outline your design.

 Mix the plaster following the package directions.

Note: *Do not pour plaster down the sink drain.* When cleaning up, let the extra plaster harden in the bucket, then knock it out of the bucket and throw it in the garbage.

Pour the plaster into a clean milk carton. When it hardens, peel off the carton.

Before you start to carve, decide what you will make. You might want to make a sketch of your design on paper before you work on the plaster.

With a toothpick, sketch out the outline of your figure. Then carve away at the block. Work on old newspapers so that you can roll up the plaster crumbs when cleaning up.

When your sculpture is finished, you can smooth the surface with a wet sponge or folded paper towel.

Carve away the plaster and smooth it into a sculpture.

In the Distance: Perspective Drawing

MATERIALS

Paper
Pencil and markers

Draw a large shape, then repeat the shape inside the large one, making each one smaller. Connect the shapes and add details. Because the shape gets smaller, it looks like it is far away.

Now you can draw hallways, arches, roads, railroads, swimming pools, tunnels, and caves. Isn't it easy?

During the Middle Ages, artists began to show things both near and far away in the same picture. Paintings before that time were more like flat, cartoon outlines and didn't show things the way we really see them. Adding perspective—showing things far and near—makes a picture look 3-dimensional and more realistic.

You can easily draw a hallway, archway, road, or garden path that shows part of it near you and part of it far away.

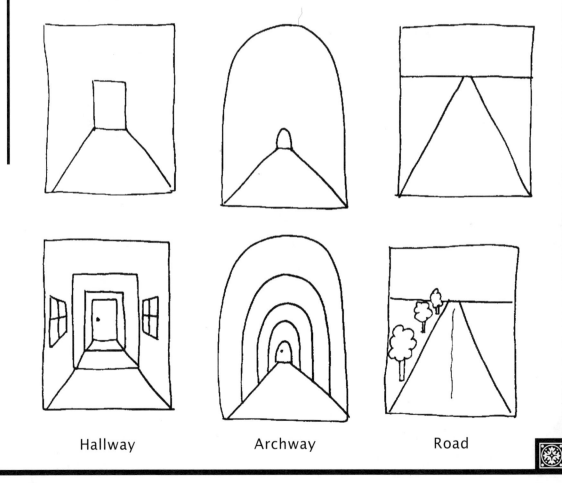

Hallway   Archway   Road

Golden Gift Box

Boxes were used to store valuable things, such as coins, jewelry, sewing tools, or books.

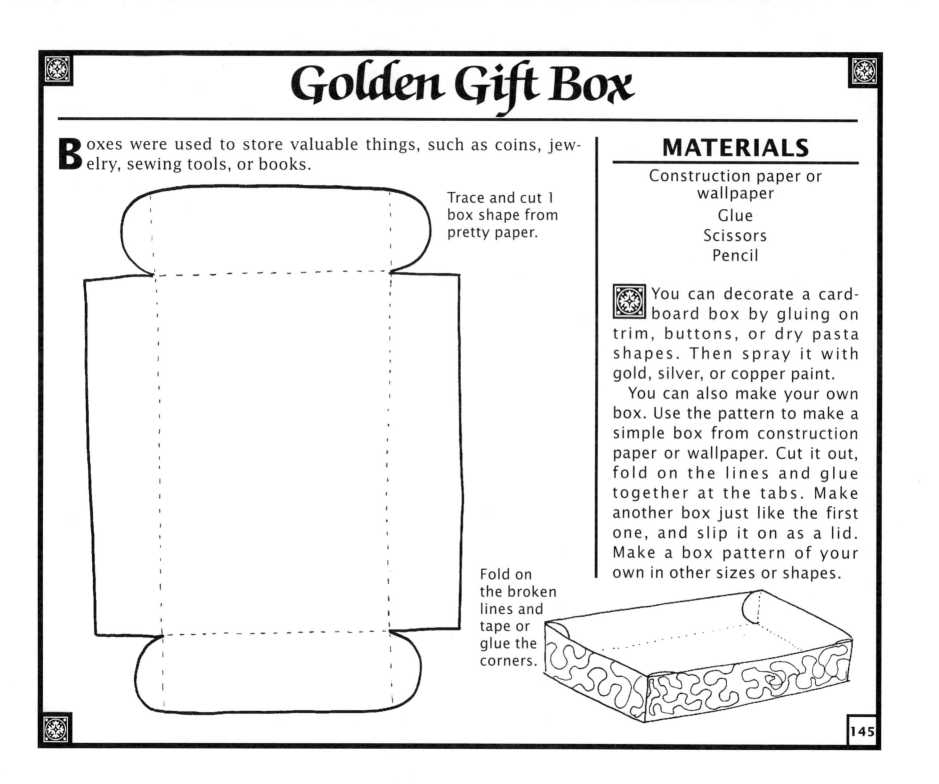

Trace and cut 1 box shape from pretty paper.

Fold on the broken lines and tape or glue the corners.

MATERIALS

Construction paper or wallpaper
Glue
Scissors
Pencil

You can decorate a cardboard box by gluing on trim, buttons, or dry pasta shapes. Then spray it with gold, silver, or copper paint.

You can also make your own box. Use the pattern to make a simple box from construction paper or wallpaper. Cut it out, fold on the lines and glue together at the tabs. Make another box just like the first one, and slip it on as a lid. Make a box pattern of your own in other sizes or shapes.

Tin Angel

MATERIALS

Disposable aluminum pie tin
Scissors
Pencil
Newspaper

Trim away the rim of the pan. Draw an angel outline in pencil. Cut it along the lines. Use a pencil or ball-point pen to press, or "emboss," a design in the metal. Do it on the back of the angel and it will show up on the front. If you work on top of a padded surface, such as folded newspaper, the design will show up better.

Fold the skirt back, the arms forward, and curve the wings

Both peasants and royalty kept religious medallions and statues in their homes.

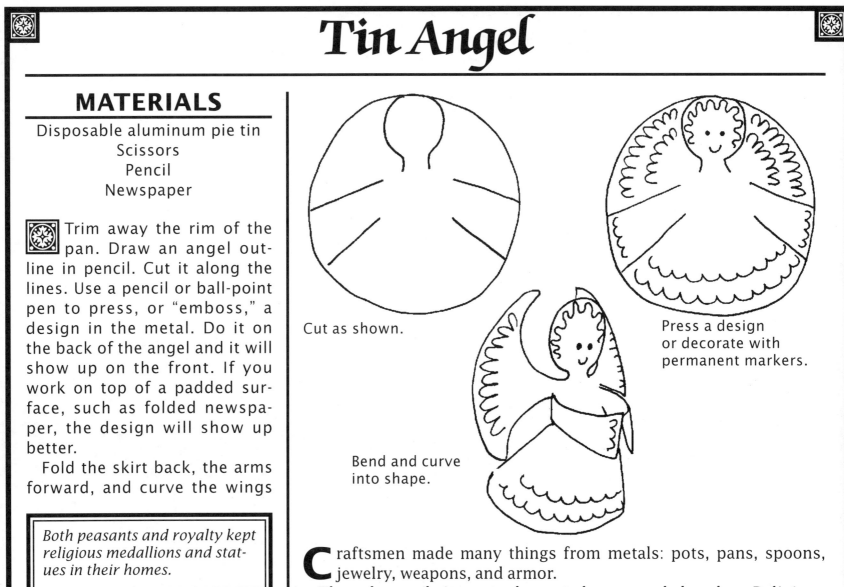

Cut as shown.

Press a design or decorate with permanent markers.

Bend and curve into shape.

Craftsmen made many things from metals: pots, pans, spoons, jewelry, weapons, and armor.

They also made items to decorate homes and churches. Religious figures were common, because the church was so important in everyone's life.

Make a little tin angel to hang from a Christmas tree or to watch over you from a shelf.

Everyday Life

Wealthy people had slaves and servants to do the work around the castle. This gave them time for reading, writing, hunting, hawking, and holding tournaments and feasts.

Common people worked in the fields or made things that they could trade. They also had to grow and prepare all their food, make their clothing, and build their furniture. As breaks from their hard lives, they had days off from work for church feast days and holy days.

Peasants in Italy worked the fields from sunup to 3 o'clock. Saturday afternoons, Sundays, and feast days were holidays, and no one worked. They had 90 holidays a year, so they had plenty of time for fairs, parades, and fun.

> *Peasants were given a flock of sheep that they took care of for several years. Then they were returned to the king, and the peasant got to keep half of the lambs as his share.*

What Time Is It?

Before people had clocks and watches, they created ways to keep track of time.

Large candles were marked to show hours passed as they burned down. Someone who woke during the night could check the burning candle and know what time it was.

Sand Glass

Sand glasses measure time by the amount of sand that runs from one end to the other. Sand glasses were used to time church sermons in medieval days.

Trace the bottle rim onto cardboard and cut it out. Use the nail to poke a tiny hole in the center of the cardboard.

Working over the bowl, fill the bottle with salt. Hold the cardboard in place and let the salt trickle out. Time the salt, and when a minute has passed, stop. Put the salt left in the bottle back in its container. Fill your bottle with the salt that went into the bowl. (You may want to use a funnel. You can make one out of aluminum foil.)

Glue the cardboard to the rims of the bottles, lining them up on top of each other. Wrap tape around them to hold them securely. When the glue dries, begin using your sand glass to time games, phone calls, cooking, or anything you want.

MATERIALS

2 small identical bottles:
drink bottles or baby food jars
Cardboard
Duct tape
Salt
Pencil
Nail
Glue
Bowl
Scissors
Clock or watch

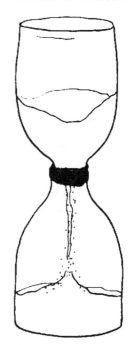

MATERIALS

2 paper plates
Scissors
Glue
Pencil

Cut away the rim from 1 plate so that it's flat.

Cut a triangle shape from the other plate.

Fold a tab in the triangle shape and glue it onto the plate, with the large end near the edge of the plate.

Go outdoors when the sun is shining. Place the sundial on a flat surface, with the end of the triangle pointing south (see how to make a compass, p. 122). Trace along the shadow with a pencil and mark the time every hour.

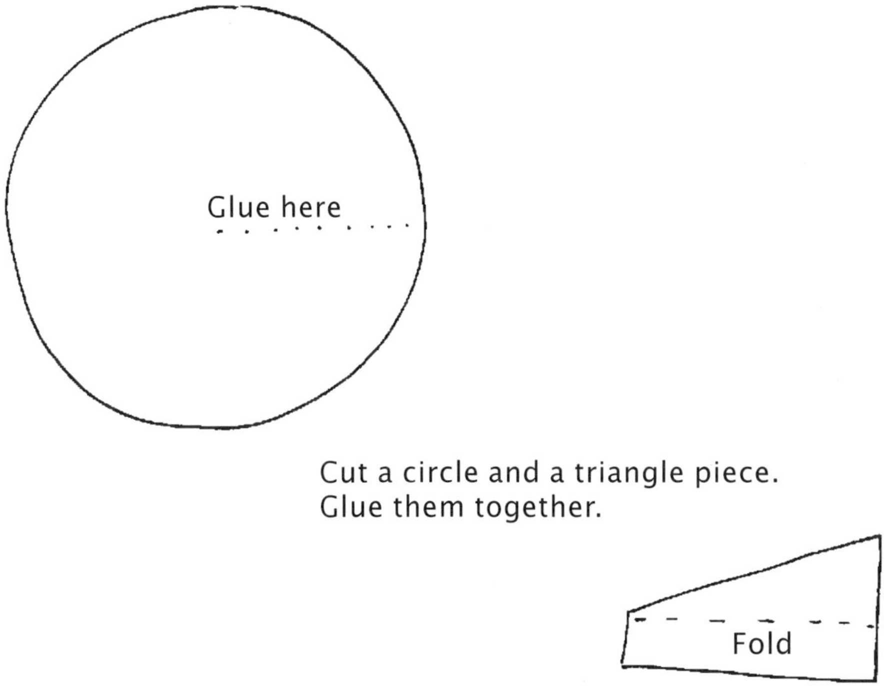

Glue here

Cut a circle and a triangle piece.
Glue them together.

Fold

Paper-Plate Sundial

A sundial tells the time of day by where its shadow falls. As the sun moves across the sky during the day, the shadow changes position on the sundial. There's only one problem: you can't tell time on a cloudy day!

Write the numbers like they did. They used Roman numbers, like these:

1 = I	7 = VII
2 = II	8 = VIII
3 = III	9 = IX
4 = IV	10 = X
5 = V	11 = XI
6 = VI	12 = XII

The numbers we use today, called Arabic numbers, came from the Arabs, who learned about them in India.

When you are done, you'll have a timepiece like those used centuries ago.

Put it in the sun and record the shadow every hour.

Dip Some Candles

Candles were the only source of light in the Middle Ages. They were made from melted animal fat (tallow) or beeswax. They were expensive, so people rarely used them unless they were wealthy.

You can make some candles, but you will need a grown-up's help. Hot wax can be dangerous because it can burn your skin or burst into flame if it gets too hot.

You can color the paraffin by dropping pieces of crayon into the hot wax and stirring it. Scented oils are made especially for candlemaking and can be purchased at craft shops. One pound of paraffin will make about 8 pairs of 4-inch candles.

Fill ⅓ of a can with water and put the can in the saucepan. Fill the saucepan half full with hot water and put it on the stove over a low heat.

Fill ⅔ of the other can with cool water, and set it aside.

Cover the work area with newspapers.

Break the wax into chunks and put it into the can of hot water. Be sure a grown-up is helping with melting the wax.

It seems strange to mix wax and water, but the wax will float on top of the water. This makes it easier for you to dip the candles, and it uses less wax.

When the wax has melted, turn the stove off.

Cut a piece of wick about 10 inches long. Hold the wick in the center and dip the ends into the melted wax. The hot wax will stick to the wick as you pull it back up, making two candles at once.

Pull the wick out of the hot wax, and dip it into the can of cold water to cool it. Repeat this. After the first two or three dips, straighten the wick by pulling it gently so your candles will be shaped nicely.

MATERIALS

Paraffin wax*

Candle wick
(from a craft supply store)

2 large soup or juice cans

Water

Saucepan

Scissors

Newspapers

*Note: You also can use old candles. They can be found in thrift stores and are often colored and scented already. Melt them as you would paraffin.

Keep dipping and cooling until the candles are the size you want. You can hang them from a nail on the wall for decoration. When you want to light them, snip the wick apart with scissors.

Dip in melted wax and then cold water. Repeat.

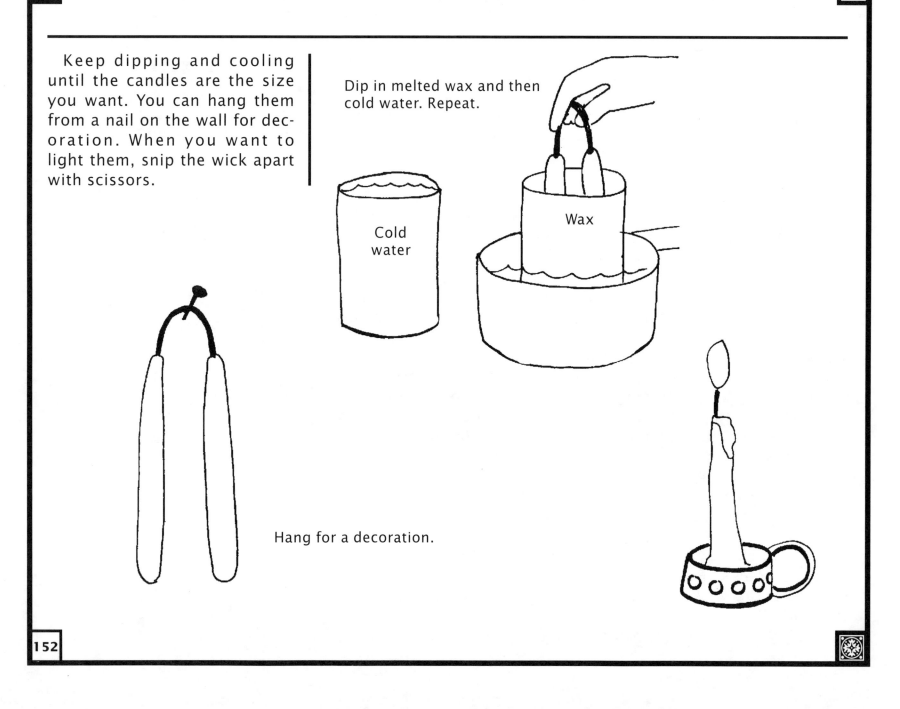

Cold water

Wax

Hang for a decoration.

Mix Some Scent

MATERIALS

Small glass jar with a lid

Virgin olive oil
(the purest kind
sold in drug stores)

Fresh flower petals

 Use rose, lilac, or verbena petals—something that smells nice. Chop up the petals and put them in the jar. Cover them with oil. Put on the lid and place the jar in a sunny windowsill. Stir or gently shake each day. After 2 weeks, strain out the petals (use a piece of old nylon stocking as a strainer). Then, fasten the lid and store your scented oil in a dark place—a cupboard or cabinet. Mmmm . . . what a nice smell!

Men shaved by rubbing whiskers off with a pumice stone.

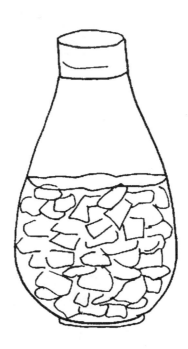

Cover torn petals with olive oil. Let it stand 2 weeks, and then strain out the petals.

In medieval days everyone wanted to smell good. They thought bad odors caused disease, so they went through all sorts of efforts to make their homes, clothes, and body smell fragrant.

Herbs were scattered on the floors, and clothing was washed in flower-scented water and packed away sprinkled with flower petals.

Everyone who could afford it wore perfumed oil. You can make some easily.

Rose Water

Flower petals were used everywhere in the Middle Ages.

Rose water was used in bath tubs, to wash hands at the table while eating, as perfume, in medicines, and even sprinkled in fountains. New babies were rolled in rose petals in order to give them a good start in life.

Rose petals were used to stuff pillows and were sprinkled in chests of clothing. Sweet rushes, herbs such as mint, irises, and other flowers were strewn on the floors. What a sweet-smelling time it must have been!

Make your own rosewater perfume or give a gift bottle to your grandma or a special aunt. It can be put in bathwater, too.

Rose water was used in making sweets and drinks, too. Huge rose gardens were planted for a supply of fresh roses.

Fill a jar with petals. Cover with water. Let soak.

Strain the petals with a nylon stocking. Store the rose water in the refrigerator.

Rose water

MATERIALS

Fresh rose petals
(ask a friendly florist for discards if you don't have any in your yard)
Water
Glass jar with lid
Old nylon stocking
Bowl

Pack the jar full of rose petals. Pour in just enough water to cover the petals. Close the lid and let the jar of petals sit in a sunny spot for 9 days. Pour the water into the bowl, using the nylon stocking to strain the petals from the water. Pour the rose water back into the small jar. Store it in the refrigerator.

What a special gift!

Herb Salts

MATERIALS

Salt

Fresh or dried herbs:
basil, chives, garlic, marjoram, oregano, rosemary, savory, tarragon, and thyme

Clean jars with lids:
baby food, instant coffee, or pickle jars

Choose a single herb or a mixture of several. Use one cup of salt to one cup of fresh, chopped herbs, or 5 to 8 tablespoons of dry herbs. You can add a sprinkle of paprika to give it some color.

If you use fresh herbs, spread them on a cookie sheet to dry. It may take a few days. Do not place the tray in the sunlight. When the herbs are dry, crush them between your fingers and mix them with the salt.

Fill, cover, and label the jars.

Herb salts are great for cooking, making garlic toast, or sprinkling on fresh vegetables.

Medieval people made salt by boiling down pans of ocean water. The salt was coarse, polluted, and colored brown, black, or green. They also dug rock salt out of mines. Only the wealthy could afford to flavor their foods with herbs. The poor soaked their dried, salted meat in garlic juice instead.

Both salt and herbs were expensive during the Middle Ages. Without them, food tasted pretty boring. Mix some of this herb blend to use at dinner, or to give as a gift.

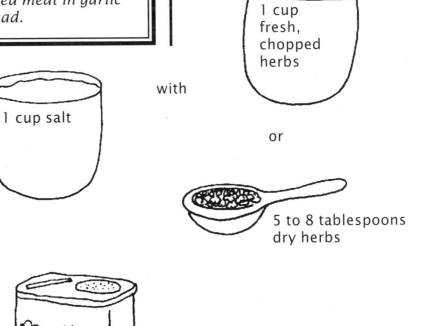

1 cup salt

with

1 cup fresh, chopped herbs

or

5 to 8 tablespoons dry herbs

Add a sprinkle of paprika for color.

Flowered Soap

The Celts of Ireland and Scotland created soap. It was made by cooking animal fat, wood ashes, and soda. Fragrant herbs were added to give it a pleasant smell.

Decorate a bar to give to someone special or to use yourself.

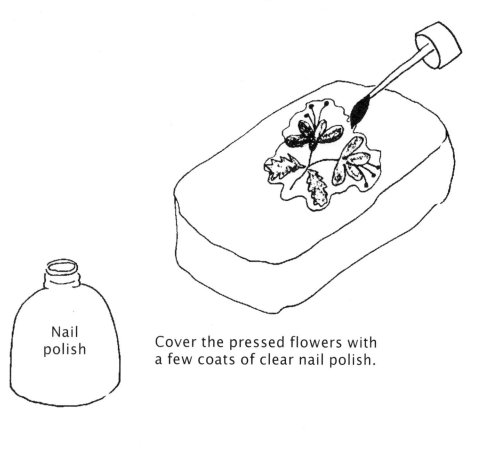

Nail polish

Cover the pressed flowers with a few coats of clear nail polish.

MATERIALS

White or pastel bar soap with a nice scent

Pressed wildflowers*

Clear nail polish

*Note: Gather wildflowers and press them between pages of a phone book until they are flat and dry. If you can't find any, clip fronds from houseplants, such as ferns, and press them between 2 sheets of typing paper with a warm iron.

Position the dry flowers on the soap. Wet them with a bit of water to make them stick. Dry them with a tissue and paint over the flowers with clear nail polish. Give the flowers several coats so that they are completely covered.

Bathtubs were shared with other people. The water was sprinkled with herbs and flowers to make it smell good.

Create Coins

MATERIALS

Styrofoam or
self-hardening clay
Aluminum foil
Scissors
Glue
Pencil
Toothpick

 You can cut coin shapes from Styrofoam. Press designs into the Styrofoam with a pencil. Wrap and glue aluminum foil over it.

Coins can be shaped from self-hardening clay. Press designs—your own likeness, perhaps—into the soft clay with a toothpick. Let it harden.

Coins weren't always round, and today some countries have coins of other shapes. Use any shape you like.

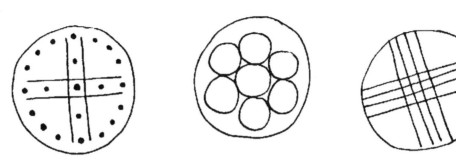

Here are some designs found on very old coins.

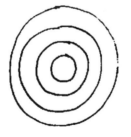 

Coins were used by the Greeks, Romans, and Celts. In the Middle Ages, coins were made from gold, silver, copper, and bronze. Kings and queens enjoyed having coins made with their name or picture on them.

To make coins, a piece of metal was marked with decorated forms (called *dies*) by striking it with a hammer.

Weigh with a Balance

A balance was used to weigh things when people were trading. It was important that valuables like gold and spices were weighed carefully, and even bread was often weighed before purchase.

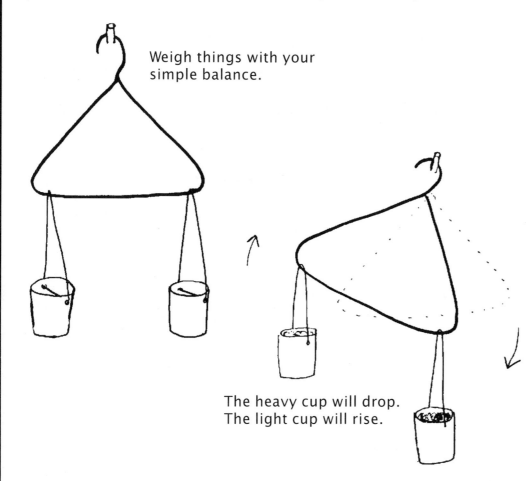

Weigh things with your simple balance.

The heavy cup will drop.
The light cup will rise.

MATERIALS

Wire coat hanger
Heavy string
2 paper cups
Pencil
Scissors

Use a pencil to poke 2 holes in the top edges of the cups. Space them across from each other.

Cut 2 pieces of string, each 15 inches long. Thread the strings through the holes in the cups and tie them to the bottom of the hanger. Slide the strings along the hanger to position each cup at an end of the hanger.

Hold your balance steady with one hand and put small items in the cups. If things weigh the same, the cups will hang level with each other. If one item is heavier, the cup will dip down.

Falconry

MATERIALS

9-by-12-inch brown or gray
construction paper
Yellow paper
Black marker
Scissors
Glue

 Make a falcon shape like the one shown.

Trace the pattern on the paper. Cut it out. Clip out the wings on the lines as shown in the illustration.

Draw eyes and other details with the marker. Glue on yellow paper for a beak. Cut out finger holes.

Fold the bird's body back along the dotted lines. Perch it on your finger, ready for the queen's hunting party.

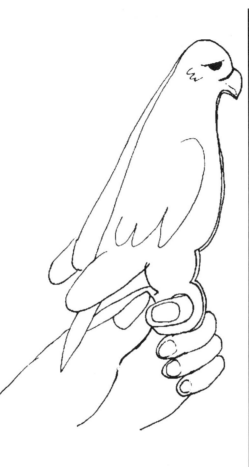

Falconry, or hawking, was enjoyed during the Middle Ages as a sport. People trained birds of prey to hunt other birds or small mammals for them. Hunting was a popular sport for wealthy lords and ladies, who owned fields and forests to hunt in.

Falcons or hawks were tamed and carried on the hunter's arm out to the field. A soft leather helmet was put over the bird's head so it couldn't see anything and wouldn't get excited. Long leather thongs were tied to their legs.

The owner would carry the bird on his or her arm out to the fields, and then remove the hood and thongs so that the bird could fly after prey.

You can perch a pretend falcon on your finger.

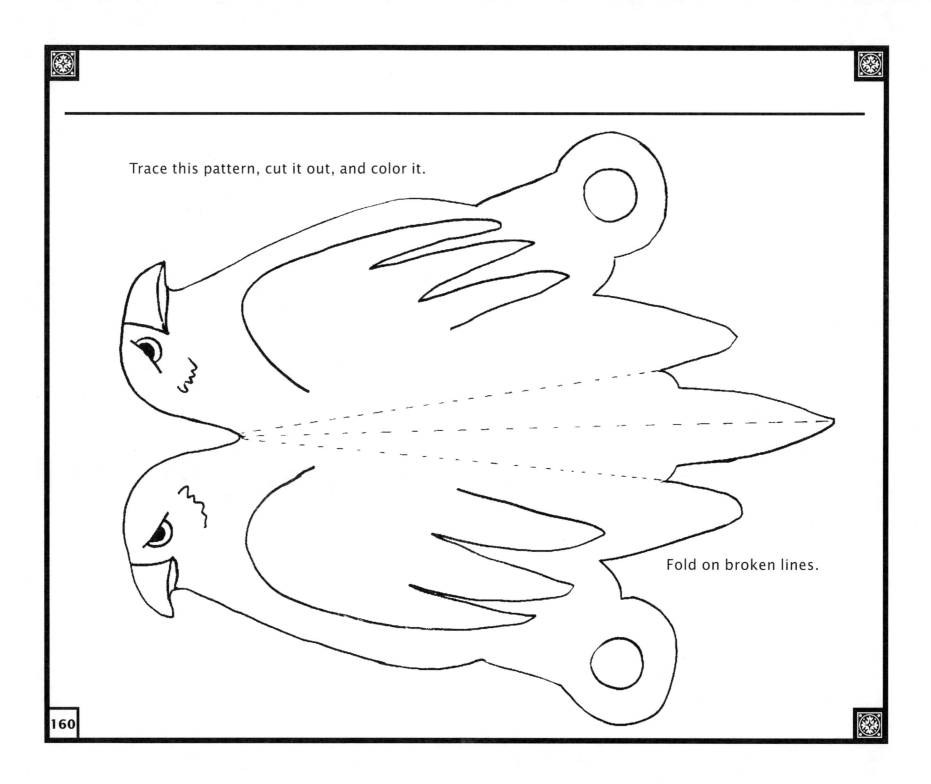

Trace this pattern, cut it out, and color it.

Fold on broken lines.

Glorious Goblet

Glue 2 cans together
to make a metal goblet.

Use it at your next feast!

MATERIALS

6-ounce tuna fish can
(make sure there are
no sharp edges)
4-ounce can
Hot glue gun or bathtub caulk

Remove the labels and wash the cans thoroughly in warm, soapy water. Dry them. Glue the cans together at their bases. You can really drink from this goblet. Make a set for everyone you're inviting to your next feast.

The village barber was also the dentist and the surgeon. He treated the sick by cutting them to make them bleed a little. People thought that illness might be caused by too much blood in the body. Of course, doctors today know that this isn't true at all.

Drinking cups were made of wood, cow or deer horns, or metal. Cups were kept near the table on a board shelf that was called a *cupboard,* a word we still use for today's kitchen cabinets.
Make a metal goblet like the ones Vikings, Celts, and Anglo-Saxons used to make toasts at banquets long ago.

Pass on Some Proverbs

Proverbs are short sayings that make a point. Here are some of the proverbs people said during the Middle Ages. Can you make up one or two about life today?

Don't count your chickens before they hatch.
means
Don't plan for something to happen, until it does.

One shears the sheep, the other the pig.
means
One person is wise, the other isn't—a pig has no wool.

He casts roses before swine.
means
He wastes effort or things on people who don't appreciate it.

He's an ear-blower.
means
He's a gossip.

The world turns on her thumb.
means
She's lucky.

It's a hoe without a handle.
means
A useless thing.

He sits in his own light.
means
He's proud of himself.

The pigs run loose in the corn.
means
Everything has gone wrong.

He kills 2 flies with one blow.
means
Gets 2 things done at once.

She takes the hen's egg and leaves the goose's.
means
Makes a bad choice—a goose's egg is bigger.

A House Is a Home

Most people lived in small cottages. They built the cottages near a castle so that the lord's knights could protect them. A wall was sometimes built around the village to keep out bandits and strangers. The gates could be closed at night. Few people lived out in the countryside because there was no protection.

Cottages were built of wood, with mud and straw plastered on the outside. Roofs were of thatch—dry bundles of grass. There was always danger from fire, so at night a bell was rung to remind everyone to cover their hearth fire and put out their candles.

Houses were small and simple. They were divided to give room for the cows, hens, and other animals to live in part of the house, too. Rich children had their own bedrooms, but most children had to share. They had to share the bed, too. Beds were large, and often six relatives slept together in one bed. (Even in inns and hospitals, people were expected to share a bed with others!)

The family bedroom was the place everyone gathered to visit, work, and say prayers. The family's valuable treasures were kept there, locked in chests.

Clothing was stored in trunks. Tools and other items were hung on the walls. The furniture was simple and made of wood.

The first homes didn't have windows, but after glass was invented they became more common. The first windows were made of small round pieces of glass held together with a framework of lead. Wooden shutters could be closed, bolted, and locked over the windows.

Castles were the safest place to live, of course. They were first simply large houses with a thick wooden wall and a ditch around them. Later they were built on a hill, with a stone wall below, and often a moat, or small lake, around them. Later they became larger, with several buildings clustered together surrounded by several stone walls.

Besides the lord and lady of the castle, there were between 10 and 200 people living inside. They all had jobs to do because running such a large house took many hands. There were gardens, storerooms, bee-hives (for honey), and henhouses. Whatever was needed had to be grown or made within the castle or village. They also had to be ready to defend the castle from armies who wanted to take it.

> *Not all castles were built of stone. Wooden castles were built, too. Not all of the kings and queens were wealthy enough to build with stone.*
>
> *The early peasant cottages didn't have chimneys. The fire was built in the center of the house and the smoke went up through a hole in the roof. It must have been very smoky inside.*

Paper-Bag Cottages

MATERIALS

Lunch-sized brown paper bag
Newspaper
Construction paper
Tape
Colored markers
Scissors
Glue

Crumple newspapers and stuff the bag about ¾ full. Tape the top closed.

Make the roof from half a sheet of 9-by-12-inch construction paper. Use the markers to draw a thatched or tiled roof. Fold it in half and glue it onto the top of the bag.

Make windows, shutters that fold open and closed, doors, and window boxes, and glue them onto the bag. Use markers to draw lines that look like stone and wood.

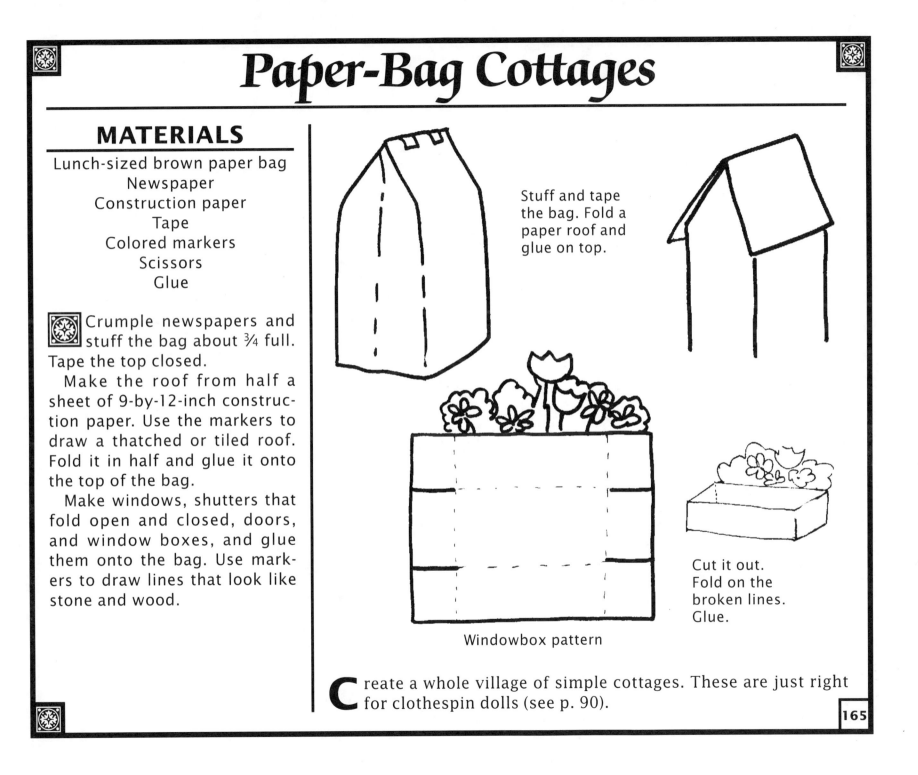

Stuff and tape the bag. Fold a paper roof and glue on top.

Windowbox pattern

Cut it out. Fold on the broken lines. Glue.

Create a whole village of simple cottages. These are just right for clothespin dolls (see p. 90).

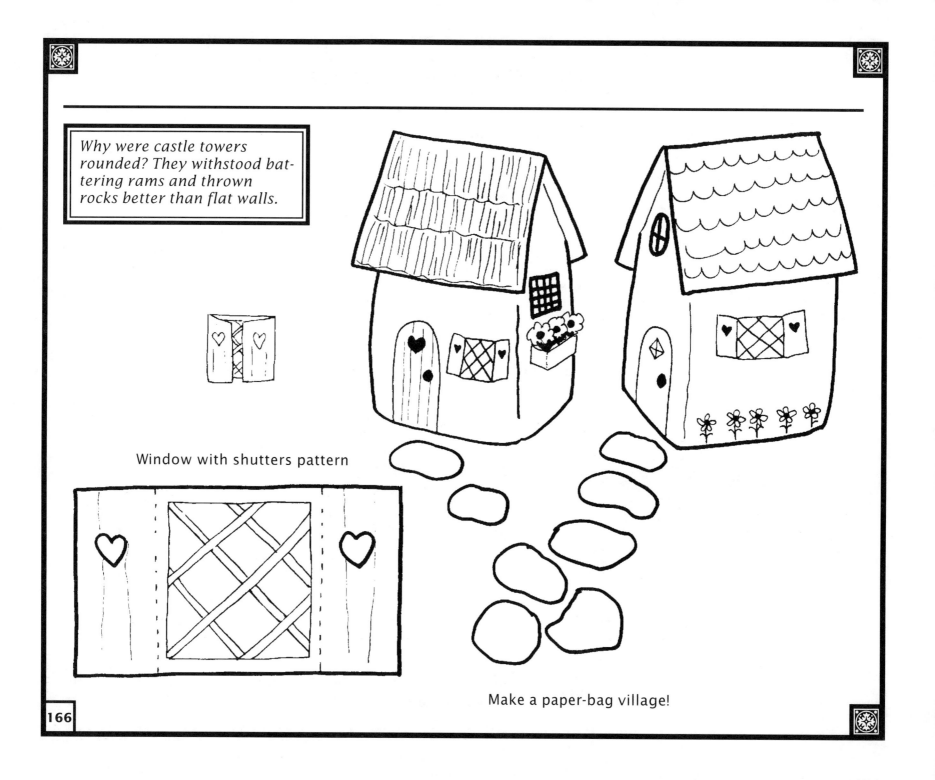

Why were castle towers rounded? They withstood battering rams and thrown rocks better than flat walls.

Window with shutters pattern

Make a paper-bag village!

Create a Castle

Here's how to make a super-simple castle. It's like the first ones—a main building surrounded by a wall.

MATERIALS

Large soup can
2 bathroom tissue tubes
6-by-9-inch cardboard
Gelatin box
(or similar small box)
Construction paper
Scissors
Tape
Glue
Markers

Cover the tissue tubes with colored construction paper. It helps to roll the paper around the tube to measure the size before cutting. Add ½ inch to the top. Cut square notches along the top. These are called "crenelations," the openings that soldiers used to shoot bows and arrows through while they hid behind the wall. Glue the paper around the tubes.

Cover the soup can with paper. Use half a sheet of 9-by-12-inch paper to make a half-circle. Roll and tape it to make a cone for the roof. Glue it to the soup can.

Cover the cardboard with colored paper. This will be the base. Glue the three towers in place.

Cover the gelatin box with colored paper, drawing on some castle gates. Glue it in front of the towers.

Make the wall by cutting two pieces of 3-by-9-inch colored paper. Glue the ends to make a long strip. Draw on stone details with markers. Fold 1 inch under. Snip slits to the fold about 1 inch apart. Use these little tabs to glue the wall to the cardboard around the towers.

Fold and glue a rectangle of paper or cloth to a coffee stirrer or drinking straw and glue it to the tower for a flag.

Use a half-circle to make the tower roof.

Make the wall.

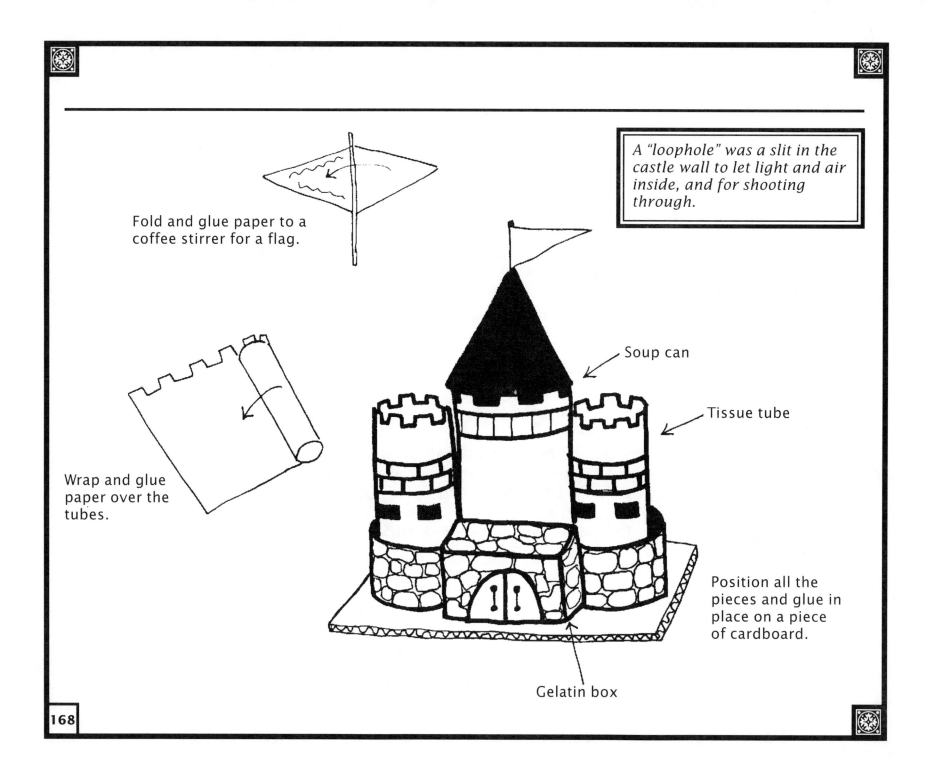

Fold and glue paper to a coffee stirrer for a flag.

A "loophole" was a slit in the castle wall to let light and air inside, and for shooting through.

Soup can

Tissue tube

Wrap and glue paper over the tubes.

Position all the pieces and glue in place on a piece of cardboard.

Gelatin box

168

Castles for Your Pocket

MATERIALS

Construction paper
Toothpicks
Pencil
Crayons
Scissors
Tape
Glue

Draw a line about 1 inch from the edge of a piece of construction paper. This will become the castle wall. Draw and color a castle in the center of the wall. Cut it out, tape the ends of the wall together. Snip a "T" shaped opening in the front wall and fold open to make castle gates. Glue tiny pieces of colored paper to toothpick pieces and glue on as flags.

While castles were the largest houses ever made, you can make them tiny enough to fit in your pocket!

Castles were built strong against attack. The most danger came from starvation during a siege, or from disloyal people within the castle.

Make cottages, too.

Glue at "X"'s.

Cut open gates and fold back.

Conclusion

The Middle Ages was an interesting time in history. People's lives changed a lot during those centuries. From simple armed forts, castles grew into villages, and towns sprang up. People began to travel, trade, and explore new ideas. Towns were growing, nations developing.

Life then was hard and dangerous, even for the rich and royal. Everyone had a job to do, and they depended on the work of others for comfort and safety. People thought that honor, courtesy, and courage were very important. People respected heroes and heroines who tried to live up to those ideals. These things are still very important today. It's fun to study the past, and explore how people once lived and solved their problems. Our lives today have been shaped and changed by history. Perhaps the activities in this book have taken you back a few steps in time to discover what life was like long ago.

Bibliography

Sources

Bayard, Tania. *A Medieval Home Companion: Housekeeping in the 14th Century.* New York: HarperCollins Publishers, 1991.

Cirker, Blanche, ed. *The Book of Kells: Selected Plates.* New York: Dover Publications, 1982.

de Corbie, William. *A Primer in Calligraphy & Illumination.* Milpitas, Calif.: Society for Creative Anachronism, 1990.

Delort, Robert. *Life in the Middle Ages.* New York: Crown Publishers, 1972.

Drogin, Marc. *Yours Truly, King Arthur: How Medieval People Wrote.* New York: Taplinger Publishing Co., 1982.

Duby, Georges, ed. *A History of Private Life: Vol. II. Revelation of the Medieval World.* Cambridge, Mass.: Harvard University Press, 1988.

Hieatt, Constance B., and Sharon Butler. *Pleyn Delit: Medieval Cookery for Modern Cooks.* Toronto: University of Toronto Press, 1976.

Holmes, George, ed. *Oxford Illustrated History of Medieval Europe.* Oxford: Oxford University Press, 1988.

Hopkins, Andrea. *Knights.* New York: Artabras, 1990.

King, Constance Eileen. *Collector's History of Dolls.* New York: Bonanza Books, 1977.

Kohler, Carl. *A History of Costume.* New York: Dover Publications, 1976 (reprint of 1928 edition).

National Geographic Society, *The Age of Chivalry,* 1969.

Lofts, Nora. *Domestic Life in England.* New York: Doubleday & Co., 1976.

de Montferrat del la Meslaye, Guy, ed. *Indoor Games (or How to While Away a Siege).* Milpitas, Calif.: Society for Creative Anachronism, 1983.

Neuschutz, Karin. *The Doll Book.* Burdett, New York: Larson Publications, 1982.

Society for Creative Anachronism, *Known World Handbook,* 1992, Office for the Stock Clerk, P.O. Box 360743, Milpitas, CA 95036-0743. (The SCA is a nonprofit educational organization that researches and recreates the customs, combat, and courtesy of the Middle Ages and the Renaissance. They have chapters all over the U.S. Write for a list of publications.)

Sokolov, Raymond. *Why We Eat What We Eat.* New York: Summit Books, 1991.

Tannahill, Reay. *Food in History.* New York: Crown Publishing, 1988.

Viola, Herman J., and Carolyn Margolis. *Seeds of Change.* Washington, D.C.: Smithsonian Institution Press, 1991.

Visser, Margaret. *The Rituals of Dinner.* New York: Grove Weidenfeld, 1991.

Children's Books

Brandenberg, Aliki. *A Medieval Feast.* New York: Thomas Crowell, 1983.

Carroll, Lewis. *Jabberwocky.* Cleveland: Modern Curriculum Press, 1987.

Dana, B. *Young Joan.* New York: Charlotte Zolotow/Harper-Collins, 1991.

Glubock, Shirley. *Knights in Armor.* New York: Harper & Row, 1969.

Goodall, J. S. *The Story of a Castle.* New York: Margaret K. McElderry Books, 1986.

Green, John. *Life in a Medieval Castle and Village: Coloring Book.* New York: Dover Publications, 1990.

Gross, Gwen (retelling). *Knights of the Round Table.* New York: Scholastic, 1985.

Hartman, Gertrude. *Medieval Days and Ways.* New York: MacMillan, 1958.

Hindley, Judy. *Knights and Castles.* London: Usborne Publishing, 1989.

Hodges, Margaret (retelling). *St. George and the Dragon.* Boston: Little, Brown, & Co., 1984.

Hunt, J. *Illuminations.* New York: Bradbury Press, 1989 (an alphabet book).

Lasker, Joe. *Merry Ever After.* New York: Puffin Books/Viking Press, 1976.

Lasker, Joe. *A Tournament of Knights.* New York: Harper & Row, 1986.

Macaulay, D. *Castle.* Boston: Houghton Mifflin, 1977.

Mayer, M. *The Unicorn Alphabet.* New York: Dial Books, 1989.

Oakes, C. *Exploring the Past: The Middle Ages.* New York: Harcourt Brace Jovanovich, 1989.

Peris, Carme; Verges, Gloria; and Oriol Verges. *The Renaissance.* New York: Barron's, 1988.

Pyle, Howard (retold by Don Hinkle). *King Arthur.* Mahwah, N.J.: Troll Associates, 1988.

Scarry, H. *Looking into the Middle Ages.* New York: Harper & Row, 1984 (a pop-up book).

Unstead, R. J. *See Inside a Castle.* New York: Kingfisher Books, Ltd., 1986.